Working My Way Through Life

Tales That Can Be Told

Russ Vahlbusch

Ideas into Books®
WESTVIEW
KINGSTON SPRINGS, TENNESSEE

Ideas into Books®
WESTVIEW
P.O. Box 605
Kingston Springs, TN 37082
www.publishedbywestview.com

Copyright © 2020 Russell Stearns Vahlbusch

All rights reserved, including the right to reproduction, storage, transmittal, or retrieval, in whole or in part in any form.

ISBN 978-1-62880-150-7

First edition, May 2020

Photo credits: Cover photo by Mark Trapani

Printed in the United States of America on acid free paper.

For

_____

Our Sons – Eric and Jeff

They having been our most important work of all.

TABLE OF CONTENTS

Foreword xi

THE WORK 1
1933: Junior Housekeeper 3
1935: Assistant Paperboy 6
1938: Paperboy 9
1940: Caddie 12
1942: Receptionist and Guide 19
1944: Gas Station Attendant 24
1945: Stock Handler 30
1946: Shoe Salesman 34
1947: House Painter 39
1948: Spot Welder 43
1949: Spray Painter 48
1949: Bookstore Clerk 53
1950: YMCA Counselor 55
1950: Busboy 59
1951: Bookstore Assistant Supervisor 64

UNITED STATES ARMY 71

1951: Infantry Trainee 73

1952: Non-Com Leadership Trainee................. 89

1952: Officer Candidate....................................... 91

1952: Combat Infantryman 97

1953: Company Clerk 121

1953: Group Insurance Salesman 137

MICHIGAN BELL TELEPHONE COMPANY . 157

1954: College Trainee 159

1955: Commercial Operations Assistant.......... 173

1956: Staff Supervisor—Methods..................... 177

1959: Order Manager—City 193

1962: Billing/Order Manager—Suburban 220

1965: Order Manager—City 232

1967: Billing Manager—City............................ 240

1968: Management Assessor 245

1968—1976: Instructor, Dale Carnegie & Associates—Moonlighting 253

1976—1979: Instructor, Wayne State University—Moonlighting 260

1969: Staff Manager—Mechanization Methods 262

1972: Instructor—Management Training 270

1975: Corporate Performance Consultant....... 279

1977: Co-Director—MBT President's Conference 284

1978: District Manager—Succession Planning 298

1979: District Manager—Management Training and Education 303

1987: District Manager—S.R. Training— Telephone Sales 328

1989–1996: Consultant—Jannotta Bray & Associates 340

Afterword...347

Acknowledgments 349

Given names and surnames in this volume are from memory and may contain misspellings. Dates may have unintended variances.

WE SPEND OUR YEARS AS A TALE THAT IS TOLD.

Psalm 90:9 KJV

FOREWORD

During the past several years I thought about writing an autobiography. After a couple of false starts I concluded that the best way to organize this effort was to tie my life to my work.

For everyone who has worked outside the home it seems like a natural way to tell one's story. This is what I have aimed to do with

Working My Way Through Life.

As this project unfolded, social, economic, and work-related issues became the story.

The Author
Chippewa Falls, Wisconsin
April 2, 2020

THE WORK

JUNIOR HOUSEKEEPER: 1933

Harriet Adele Vahlbusch (née Stearns) was my mother. She ran what in those days was often referred to as *a tight ship*. She talked it over with my father, and they decided that I should have an allowance. For this five-year-old they settled on twenty-five cents per week. This was to help teach me—in their words—to value work and money.

They assigned me three jobs and explained them all at one time. The first was the carrying out of disposable garbage. We lived at 87 Grove Avenue in Highland Park, Michigan. Behind every home in the city was a wide, cement-paved alley. That was Henry Ford's idea. After all, his auto plants dominated the landscape. In back of each garage was a standard-sized, city-approved, metal garbage can with a tight-fitting lid. Twice each week (three times in the summer), a city-owned garbage truck would traverse the alleys, emptying all the garbage cans.

Household garbage (not trash) was carefully wrapped in several layers of newspaper. Externally, the resulting packages resembled a very large wrapped sub sandwich from today's marketplace. My daily task was to carry these packets out the alley gate, across the back of the garage, remove the tight-fitting can top, deposit the packet, and replace the lid firmly. No problem.

I never forgot to perform this task as defined, and on time.

My second job was in the bathroom. My "boss" had a certain way towels and washcloths were to be folded. Edges had to be turned in upon themselves, so that both exposed sides of the fabric were on a fold. Then the folded towel had to be placed squarely on the towel bar.

The third job involved my clothes, when headed for the washing machine. These were to be placed in the white-painted wicker hamper, which was located in the bathroom; they were never to be left on the floor of my bedroom or closet.

Although I never missed a garbage assignment or a clothes-hamper placement, towel folding was a bit different. I sometimes forgot. Plus, I did not see this as an essential task, like handling potentially smelly garbage. However, at five years of age my vision of what was important changed when a fine of five cents was levied upon each improperly folded towel or wash cloth. That amounted to five rolls of caps for my "Tom Mix" six-shooter.

If such fines for a five-year-old child made me neurotic, so be it. Years later, when I was drafted into the army, I soon found out that keeping my footlocker shaped up would mean a weekend pass for me on inspection day. I often smiled, remembering how my first "top sergeant" had taught me the need for neatness and organization.

☙

ASSISTANT PAPERBOY: 1935

Bob Liddell was my neighbor. He was twelve years old. I was seven. He had a paper route for the largest daily in Michigan—*The Detroit News*. He had circa forty-four subscribers, covering three city blocks. Bob invited me to help him collect his route, which he did every Saturday morning. Credit cards and annual subscriptions were far into the future.

I accepted his offer. Payment was an ice cream treat at the Brown's Creamery soda fountain in Highland Park, Michigan, our hometown. Payment choices included a tin-roof sundae or a malted milk. In summer, I could substitute one-half of a scooped-out cantaloupe melon filled with a scoop of French vanilla ice cream. It was always my summer selection.

The "work" was easy. I worked one side of the street, going to each customer's front door. In the beginning most customers would say, "You are not my paperboy." I would simply reply, "I am helping my friend Bob," and point across the street. He would wave and the collection was made.

It was very exciting for a seven-year-old to wear a money changer. This device contained tubes for quarters, dimes, nickels, and pennies. With the flick of a little lever, a single coin would pop out the bottom of the proper tube into your hand, whenever it was necessary to make change.

Home delivery of the daily and Sunday cost fifteen cents a week—the six dailies were twelve cents and Sunday three cents. Some subscribers chose to pay every other week, so all in all, there was quite a bit of change to be made for dollar bills and fifty-cent pieces (a coin more commonly in use back then). Customers knew better than to tender any currency denomination above one dollar.

I loved wearing and using that money changer. It was the best part of the job.

Two weeks before Bob was to go on vacation with his family, we would switch sides of the street so all customers would get to know me. Each customer was represented by a long cream-colored card that hung on a wire ring carried by the collector. The cards contained fifty-two circled numbers to be punched out by the carrier when each weekly payment was received. Metal paper punches also hung from our belts. *The Detroit News* rules said that I was not old enough to deliver newspapers, so the station supervisor filled in for that task during vacations. However, there were no rules on how old one needed to be to handle the cash.

This cash-only system worked fine back then. The carrier had to collect enough to pay the weekly bill, which was received from the sub-station supervisor where Bob picked up his papers each day. The bills were prepared by the district manager, who had many rented garage-based sub-stations in his (never her) territory. Often the carrier had payments left outstanding from people on vacation or not home on Saturday morning. Some just did not answer the door, even though we knew they were home. Thus, my friend Bob often had to do a bit of after-school collecting on weekdays in order to realize his profit. That was not part of my job.

‌‌‌

‌‌

CB

PAPERBOY: 1938

The *Highland Parker* was the only weekly newspaper in our hometown, which was located in southeast Michigan. The staff was known for sound reporting of local news and events. Their coverage of high school sports was considered to be exemplary. Later, when I was a high school student, a fellow classmate named Jim Ferns, a varsity basketball player, had a sports byline in the *Parker*.

But I digress. I saw an ad for a carrier in the paper. I applied and got the job delivering about fifty papers every Thursday after school. My route was in the northwest corner of the city, and included a small three-story apartment building that housed twelve units.

The task of delivering this paper was a modest one. The papers were thin, easily carried in a regular-sized canvas newsboy bag. I only felt the need to change shoulders halfway through the route.

The task of collecting for the paper was not only a difficult one, but also, in my opinion—then and still—a very weird assignment. The *Highland*

Parker was a *free* publication. However, carriers were required to visit and attempt to collect from every "subscriber."

We were given a 3" x 3" pad of serially numbered "Paid in Full" receipts, to give to customers who paid the ten-cent-per-week fee. I was trained to speak face-to-face with each customer as follows: *Be confident and say "Collect for the Highland Parker."* Most of the time the response was "I thought the paper was *free*." My trained answer was "It is, but when you pay, you receive a receipt." I was then to show the customer the receipt pad. Circa one-half of those customers did then, in fact, pay the ten cents and took the receipt. The other one-half said "no thanks."

My pay for doing the weekly delivery was $.75, including these collection attempts. Collections averaged $2.50.

It seemed a little weird for a free paper, but the company not only got the delivery paid for, via those collections, but cleared $1.75 as well. After a few months, my pay was raised to $1.00 (a fortune for a ten-year-old). I like to think this was because I collected more "ten cents" than many of the other carriers—as confirmed by the number of receipts I issued—though no one ever told me that.

Fast-forward fifty-seven years to 1995. While preparing for our 50th high school reunion, our committee visited the Highland Park public library to peruse archived copies of *Highland Parker* newspapers from our high school days (1942—1945). The publisher back then had captured high school events very well. We were able to make numerous poster-sized photos of classmates and happenings from those now-nostalgic times. Even though I only delivered the *Highland Parker* for two years—and did so four years before I was even in high school—I still felt some ownership of the photos from that newspaper.

☙

CADDIE: 1940

The Detroit Golf Club was a high-end private country club located within the city limits of Detroit, Michigan. It bordered on my home town of Highland Park.

I had played golf only a few times, always with my friend and neighbor Don Thompson. I had a few clubs, all wooden shafts, given to me by my uncles Art and Wally when they purchased new ones with metal shafts. The course we played was named Palmer Park. It was public, flat, and dry.

A friend of mine named Bill Maddel was a caddie at this private club. He was fourteen years old and had begun caddying at age twelve, when boys were able to try out. I asked Bill what I needed to do to begin the trial. He did not know, but said that I should contact the caddie master, Mr. Hugh Syron, to find out what to do. So I looked Mr. Syron up in the huge Detroit telephone book (Yellow Pages were still included in those days). I found the right person. Actually, he lived in an apartment near where my great-grandmother lived. For some reason that made me feel more comfortable in calling him.

I dialed the number for Mr. Syron. After a few rings, a man answered. He did not sound very friendly. I blurted out who I was, and that I would like to try out to become a caddie—and with what breath I had left, asked how I should start. Mr. Syron yelled at me over the phone, "Good God kid, does your Dad like to be called at home?" For lack of something better to say, I answered, "No." He said, "OK, be at the clubhouse at 8:00 A.M. sharp, the Monday after Easter." My profuse thank-you was lost. Mr. Syron had hung up.

I reported ten minutes early. Mr. Syron said a few words, not really of welcome, to the assembled mass of perhaps fifty boys. We were turned over to Hugh Syron Jr. He was a college student working as assistant caddie master and pro-shop employee for the summer. It turned out that he was an outstanding golfer, and the best possible person to teach young men. He was patient, understanding, and helpful, with criticism always given in a diplomatic, developmental manner.

So, Monday through Saturday of Easter week 1940, come rain, shine, wind, etc., we trekked around those two eighteen-hole courses. Hugh Jr. and two of his helpers (senior caddies from prior years) played some serious golf. We took turns caddying. We were learning under real conditions: taught about each club, how to spot golf-balls as they were driven off the tee or from fairway or rough, how to scrub and dry golf-balls, how to wipe off club faces. We were taught protocol for holding the flag, being certain the person putting or pitching wanted it in, or out. Tryouts ended Saturday morning, with a review of the week's instruction. We had a pancake breakfast in the clubhouse. Those who were asked to attend received a plastic covered Detroit Golf Club badge with a number. My number was 282. I would begin by sitting near the end of the caddie bench.

We received a really nice cream-colored polo shirt with a Detroit Golf Club logo (DGC); we could purchase additional shirts for $1.50 each. I bought two for when I caddied several days in a row, which I frequently did. The material washed very well, including accepting Fels-Naptha soap when needed, to remove stains caused by golf bag straps on sweaty shoulders.

When I arrived at the "mile long" caddie bench first thing in the morning, I had to find my bench place based on my number. Once the bench had been set, late comers—no matter their number—joined the bench on the end. During the two summers I caddied, I was moved up gradually, based on the number of "loops" (the name given to either a nine-hole or eighteen-hole round) plus appraisals from members for whom I had worked. I reached Badge 16. This meant that for most of my second year I got a loop quite quickly, enhancing the chance that I could get a second one that same day.

This was a great job, except when caddies were in short supply. Then occasionally you were asked to "pack double." That was very hard work, but when the round was over, the money was substantial. Regular pay as a Class A caddie was $1.10 for each eighteen-hole loop or $.65 for nine holes, plus big tips of "sympathy" from the members who recognized how tough it was to carry two bags, both with a full set of clubs and an umbrella in each.

The third day I went to caddie at the club and sat on the bench, I had moved up close to the front and was about to be assigned a loop. One of the experienced caddies who had played golf during the training week approached me and said, "Have you turned on the bunker lights yet?" I said, "No, should I have?" He said, "You are the newest one here right now, and someone has to do it." He told me where to find the "toggle switch" in back of the caddie-house. So, I went in search. You guessed it; when I came back I had lost my spot on the bench. I had a lengthy wait for the next loop. It was all part of the game. No bunker lights; no toggle switch whatever that was, or is.

When beginning a new job there are always many details to learn about and decide on, other than non-existent "bunker lights." Whenever I began any new job, assignment, or venture, my dad never failed to say, "Well, you will have to find out which way the water faucets turn." I figured out early on that he was not talking about water.

It was seventeen long blocks from our house to the caddie house—about three-quarters of a mile. Should I ride my red-and-white, Roll-Fast bicycle with the balloon white-side-wall tires and a horn that was activated by the inside of my left knee? Or should I, as my maternal grandmother told me, use "shanks' mare"? I looked it up in the dictionary, and found out that meant your feet and legs. I usually biked. With my first day's income from being a caddie, I visited Mr. Thompson's record store, on Woodward Avenue near my home, to buy a 12" 78 RPM recording of Ferde Grofe's "Grand Canyon Suite" for $.90. I had caddied for eighteen holes—my card signed for the standard Class B caddie fee of $.95, plus a nice $.25 tip.

I got to caddie for Detroit Mayor Jefferies and his wife on several occasions. Ladies' day was Tuesday, on the south course. Women and caddies were not allowed to play the north course. Caddies' day was Monday. The north course was very difficult, much older and more prestigious than the south course. A sample of other interesting golfers for whom I caddied includes Freddie West, VP of American Airlines; Circuit Court Judge Chenault; Mr. Young, President/Owner of L.A. Young Spring Steel & Wire; Mr. Ponting, VP of the *Detroit News.*

The most memorable personage I encountered in this job was that of poet, philosopher, and newspaper columnist Edgar A. Guest. One Sunday I was fortunate to caddie for Mr. Guest. I had read his column in the *Free Press*, and felt honored. When the loop ended, he asked me if I would be willing to caddie for him for nine holes every Tuesday, at 3:30 P.M. He lived on the golf course in a large white brick house. I said yes, and did that for most of two golf seasons, going directly from my grade school to the course. He confided in me that he considered those nine holes his practice round, so he would be more competitive with his Sunday golfing buddies. At the end of the golf season in Michigan, the Club put on a banquet for caddies; Mr. Guest was present as the guest speaker.

He included one of his many poems about golf in his talk. He encouraged us to stay in school as long as possible. He shook hands with each caddie and thanked us for our summer of good work. Each caddie received a gift. He presented me with a plaid all-wool Mackinaw. I wore it with pride for many moons.

ଓଃ

RECEPTIONIST AND GUIDE: 1942

My paternal aunt, Lillian Elizabeth Vahlbusch (later McVay), worked at the *Detroit News* radio station, WWJ. She had been educated as a bookkeeper. She was responsible for keeping Joe Conway, the superintendent of buildings, informed of any WWJ building repairs needing attention. His office was across the street in the main *News* building.

Hence "Aunt Lil" knew of job openings in her friend Joe's department. He was looking for some young men to hire as receptionists and guides. These openings were occurring often because high school seniors and college students were being drafted into—or were enlisting in—the armed services. She asked me if I would like to apply for one of these part-time positions. I was only fourteen, but with working papers from the county, certain jobs could be approved for so-called underage workers. I obtained proper papers.

I was interviewed by Mr. Conway, and hired. The hours were 4:00 P.M. to 9:00 P.M. every

Tuesday evening, to help with the live radio audience in the 340-seat WWJ auditorium. The program being aired from 5:30 P.M. to 6:00 P.M. was a German band sponsored by the Tivoli Brewing Company.

In addition, I was assigned to the WWJ reception desk from 2:00 P.M. to 8:00 P.M. every other Sunday. Twice each month, a small ensemble from the Detroit Symphony Orchestra broadcast live from the auditorium. The conductor was Karl Kreuger; the performance occasionally featured Misha Kottler, a well-known pianist. There were regular ushers. My only responsibility to the Symphony was to help the conductor into his tails. Heady stuff at fourteen.

For this position I had to wear a sport jacket, shirt, and tie. I kept the coat and tie in the WWJ lobby cloak room so I did not need to haul these from home. The jacket I used for the entire time I worked on that job came from my cousin John Alexander, who had outgrown it. It was a fine garment of blue tweed with a half-belt across the back, purchased from a high-end store in Buffalo, N.Y. The shirts and tie came from United Shirt, just down the street from the radio station: white broadcloth with metal spring-loaded collar stays. Shirts were $.99 each. Stays $.29. Tie $.49.

My pay rate was $.65 per hour. There was no premium for Saturday or Sunday work. So, every other week I received a check for $13.59. No income tax deduction. However, there was a 5.5% ($.71) deduction for FICA. I was very solvent. Expenses were minimal. With my Highland Park junior high school bus pass, I rode the Detroit Street Railway (DSR) system (bus or street car) for six cents. I did not carry a lunch to this job. Bertram's drug store was one block away, with famous thick malts; both Lafayette and American Coney Island restaurants were five blocks away; Gus's Greek restaurant was on the corner, only two stores away from the WWJ building, with excellent American fries. Hence, carrying a brown bag was unthinkable.

During summer my hours were doubled. Plus, I was assigned to daytime shifts, on weekdays only. That is when I got to know the radio announcers and management staff. They were all interesting, especially Victor Linfoot, who went on to NBC in New York as staff announcer for Kay Kyser's world-renowned band "Kollege of Musical Knowledge." Other announcers included Ann Collins, Frank Roland, station manager Harry Bannister, and assistant manager Forrest

Wallace. Each of these people contributed to making this job a serious learning experience.

Summer also brought a new experience. I was trained to take the public on tours of the *Detroit News* plant, located across the street from the radio station. I also acted as a receptionist in that cavernous lobby. In the center of the large, high-domed ceiling space sat a knee-hole desk. That was the rallying point every Tuesday and Thursday afternoon. Group tours were scheduled at 1:00 P.M. and 3:30 P.M. Scouts, both Boy and Girl, plus school groups, from first grade through high school, arrived in the lobby, and the tours began. I was given a black, official-looking, loose-leaf binder to study. It contained descriptions of each stop on the tour of the building. My boss, Mr. Conway (never call him Joe), took me on the entire tour twice. Then I was on my own. I learned the spiel, and really enjoyed explaining how newspapers were produced, usually to eager young minds.

One other advantage of my time at this job were the many free lunches in the excellent subsidized cafeteria in the *Detroit News* building. My dad worked in that building for fifty years, minus eleven days. He was always ready to buy me lunch, whenever we were both working. Fantastic meat loaf and Hubbard squash.

One other heady experience for a fourteen-year-old was being trained to use a teargas gun. One of these defensive weapons was located under each of the reception desks in both the WWJ and *Detroit News* lobbies. Mr. Conway took a gun—and me—to the huge garage that housed the multitude of delivery trucks. They were all gone on deliveries. He demonstrated how to use the gun, shooting a tiny amount of spray into the air. Several times, I got to shoot one. Happily, I never had to use this deterrent. However, I was ready.

ℭ

GAS STATION ATTENDANT: 1944

Donald Thompson (Donny) was my first friend. His family lived across the street from us, on Grove Avenue, in Highland Park, Michigan. He was born three months before I was. We began playing together when we were four years old. We went through many stages of play as we grew up—marbles, kick-the-can, duck on the rock, tree climbing (he climbed, I watched), ball and jacks, baseball—first with soft rubber ball, then tennis ball, then softball, then hardball. We attended Saturday matinee movies together at both the Palmer Park and Uptown theaters, and on and on.

When we were both sixteen Donny asked me if I would like to spend the summer working at a gas station in Berkley, Michigan, the second suburb north of ours. My parents agreed. We started working the Monday after the last day of school in early June. This was a full-service, Sinclair brand, gas station: green, white, and red with the dinosaur logo. It was owned by Donny's brother-in-law, Verne Raymoure, who had two years remaining on a four-year enlistment in the

United States Marine Corps. Verne's dad, Verne, Sr., was running the business for his son.

Our hours and days were 8:30 A.M. to 5:30 P.M. Monday through Friday, and occasionally on Saturday. We were closed on Sunday. The location was at Twelve-Mile Road and Woodward Avenue, exactly six miles north of our homes. We could ride the interurban bus line. This was a new experience. When you entered the bus, you bought a ticket, which was punched for the distance you would be travelling and priced accordingly. We were used to one fare, no matter how far you were traveling, including free transfers, on the Detroit bus and streetcar line.

We arrived for our first day of work. There were three major parts to the job.

First was the driveway. This meant that when an auto drove in and stopped at one of the pumps, we were to drop whatever we were doing and get to the driver's side window promptly, to determine the customer's wishes. We had to keep a sharp eye out for autos, since those little black rubber tubes on the driveway which ring a bell had not yet been invented.

Second was the garage. One bay contained a hoist for grease jobs, oil changes, and tire repairs. The other bay was for everything else, especially for auto washes. We learned to do each task and were then set to work when jobs arrived. We did a bit of everything, but we washed vehicles, and then washed, and then washed some more. Part of the reason for this car wash load was because the station was located catty-corner from the world-renowned Shrine of the Little Flower Catholic Church, where the even more renowned Father Charles Coughlin held forth for several decades. The Church owned three limousines, all of which were serviced at our little station. In addition, directly across Twelve-Mile Road was the entrance to the extensive Roseland Park Cemetery. This enterprise owned four limousines. We serviced these vehicles as well. In those days, seven out of ten automobiles had wide white-sidewall tires. These seven large limousines were no exception. That summer we wore out many stiff brass-bristled brushes keeping the tire sides white. Amazingly, our arms and hands just got stronger, and did not wear out. Word got around the parish that the Sinclair station crew did a pretty good wash job. Plus, all those limos were brought in to be washed after every trip, whether they needed it or not.

We also repaired tires (very demanding work), lubed and changed oil, and worked the driveway all day long. We pumped gas (no device to keep the gas line open; all nozzles hand held), washed every windshield, asked each customer if he or she would like the oil level checked (most did), we added oil, bulk or can if needed. In addition, upon request, we cheerfully washed the rear window and often all side windows as well. When tires looked like they might need air, we checked and pumped them up.

Third was office work, keeping track of money and an occasional credit card slip.

A vital task was counting, filing, totaling, and packaging gas rationing stamps. Selling gas was very complicated during those war days. Keeping records was the way to stay in business. Most customers could not just drive up and say "fill 'er up." Rather, the number of gallons requested had to be backed up by the equivalent number of ration stamps, or a certified sticker number in the rear window, driver's side. Ration stamps per week were valued as follows: A–3 gallons; B–8 gallons; C, T, and X were special designations, including trucks. They usually meant unlimited gallons. The attendant needed to have the stamps in hand before pumping. Every gallon had to be supported by stamps when the next Sinclair tank truck arrived to fill the underground tanks, or they would remain empty. We had to carefully negotiate with customers, asking them to check their gas gauge. In the worst possible case:

Customer gives us three A-stamps, worth nine gallons. Their tank would then only take seven gallons to top it off. Customer loses two gallons, because part of that precious ration stamp could not be redeemed. The number of times we had to explain to customers to always order fewer gallons to protect them from that unhappy ending became legion.

Also included in the office work category was making certain that the customer restrooms were tidy. They were located on the south side of the building. A sign on each door read "Restroom—Key in Office." Both keys were on one-foot-long dowels, one painted blue and the other pink, with no other identification. Just choose a door. The staff had an inside facility, which everyone was told to keep neat and tidy. We did.

Our rate of pay was $.60 per hour, plus $.25 for each carwash. We tried to take turns washing, as there was money to be made. The wash also included treating the interior floor and seats with a whisk broom. Unfortunately, there was no extra charge for white sidewalls.

We felt we made decent money, and we learned a lot. Drank Cokes, from a large red ice chest embossed with *Coca Cola*. The iceman delivered two big blocks of ice every summer morning. Customers could buy one of those little original green shapely bottles of Coke for ten cents. We only had to pay five cents. That drink went well with our brown bag lunches. There was no refrigeration on site, so peanut butter and jelly got a heavy workout all summer long.

At the end of the summer, we agreed we would be willing to do it again the next summer. That did not happen. The war ended seven months later. Verne Jr. was discharged early from the Marines. He came home, and sold his gas station back to the Sinclair Oil Corporation. Verne Sr. continued his interrupted retirement. I don't know where the church and the cemetery had their limousines serviced thereafter.

૭ઝ

STOCK HANDLER: 1945

The Alemite Corporation was (and is) a large worldwide company specializing in grease guns, grease fittings, and grease. There was a small branch warehouse in my hometown of Highland Park. It was located less than a mile from our home. I had just graduated from high school and my father was ill with Meniere's disease, too dizzy to walk or work. I enrolled in Highland Park Junior College for the upcoming fall semester. This junior college was located on the west end of the block that contained both the junior and senior high schools where I had gone during the past five years.

The first summer job that I found listed in the *Highland Parker* want ads was for a "stock handler" at the Alemite corporation.

I walked over to their building, located one block to the rear of the Sherwin Williams paint store and lumber yard complex, on Hamilton Avenue. I had an interview with the office manager. He sent me into the warehouse to talk with my potential boss, the foreman, Mr. Allen.

He had to agree with the interviewer that I would do. He did.

I began working the very next day. Pay was $1.25 per hour. No work on Saturday, Sunday, or holidays. 8:00 A.M. to 4:30 P.M. daily. No overtime.

We got a thirty-minute unpaid lunchtime at our workbenches or outside on the company break bench, and two fifteen-minute paid breaks—one in the morning, one in the afternoon. Brown bagging was a must, since there were no eateries nearby, and no food wagon.

My first work assignment had a provocative description. I would be sorting, counting, and packaging nipples. This involved a variety of grease gun fittings for automobiles, classified as original equipment. For some reason many thousands of diverse fittings had been manufactured and accidently mixed, then packaged together. My first three weeks at Alemite were spent sitting on a high stool at a greasy wooden workbench under strong light, sorting a multitude of grease-gun fittings. Once this task was completed, I was assigned to the order/storage/shipping team. This meant filling orders for all products handled by this facility, plus storing new inventory as it was delivered from diverse manufacturing units located around the world.

These tasks were interesting: learning about a multitude of Alemite products involved in greasing of automobiles, tractors, airplanes, and much other machinery with moving parts. The bad day each week was Thursday. At 2:00 P.M., a semi truck carrying drums of grease arrived. It never missed a date, and was never late.

The standard packaging of grease was in fifty-five-gallon drums, weighing circa four hundred fifty pounds each. Heavy and unwieldy, the drums were rolled down a ramp off the rear of the semi. The descending speed was controlled by a strap-like harness. Not a problem. The problem was controlling the drum while rolling it to the storage area some fifty feet from the rear of the truck, and then popping it upright. These fifty-five-gallon beauties were always loaded on the rear of the truck, and came out first. We were a team of three stockmen. We each had to handle between three and five of these big drums each week, depending on the size of the order. No one ever asked us what part of our job we disliked the most. Everyone knew the answer. When the so-called specialized drums, only thirty-gallons, came down the ramp, it was such a relief that we all felt like celebrating and often did, taking an extra break time to do it. We were never asked about taking this break. In fact, our foreman never seemed to be around on drum delivery day. This was the most dangerous job I had ever held.

After one year of illness, my dad recovered, though he was now totally deaf in one ear and partially deaf in the other. I started Highland Park Junior College, and did not seek another job until the next summer—1946.

ଓଃ

SHOE SALESMAN: 1946

Mailing Brothers Shoes was a multistate retail shoe store chain for women's shoes. One store was located in downtown Detroit, directly across the side street from the famous J. L. Hudson Company, a huge twelve-story department store.

My friend Jim Key's uncle had a connection with the local owner of this very successful retail shoe business. He was looking for two young men to become temporary, full-time shoe salesmen during the summer months when regulars were taking vacations. Jim agreed to sign on, and invited me to join him.

We began our training on Saturday, three weeks before Easter. We were trained by two of the assistant store managers, in the back room among extensive shelves of shoes. We learned how to quickly determine if a particular model, size, and color was in stock. We had an introduction to the inventory. We learned how to write up special orders, and to determine if a custom shade could be dyed to match a particular gown. Often the gown was brought to the store in a big box.

We were given a company shoehorn with the embossed "MBS" logo. We were shown how to twirl this instrument skillfully. The "twirl" was the worldwide symbol of professional shoe salesmen. When there were no customers at the moment, one stood—never sat—and twirled the shoehorn on an index finger. It took practice, but in time we became quite adept with either hand.

Then we went up front, to train where real customers were shopping for shoes. The instructor waited on several customers, so we could observe and listen. He asked each customer if she was OK with helping us learn. Amazing to me at the time, every customer said yes with real enthusiasm. We learned quickly, and were soon allowed to begin meeting customers at the front door. Lots of customers were available, all in a pre-Easter shopping mood.

Mailing Brothers had a strict sales protocol. A customer must never be "walked." That term meant that if the salesman was not able to close the sale, he must turn the customer over to an assistant manager to give it a try. This employee was for certain much more experienced in closing sales. If, heaven forbid, the assistant manager was not successful, he must turn the customer over to the manager before she was allowed to "walk."

The customers did not seem to mind this. It seemed to me these high-pressure tactics should have turned them off, but I never saw or heard anyone complain or walk out in disgust.

Selling shoes was a very physical job, requiring many trips to and from the stockroom to retrieve particular models/colors/sizes, many trips up and down a four-step ladder to reach the top-tier shelves, many walks back to the customer, then much kneeling, standing, kneeling. Which shoe to purchase was often a long, drawn-out decision for many of the ladies we served. We were on our feet and on the move all day.

Mailing Brothers Shoes were mid-priced to low-priced. Often entire bridal parties would arrive to purchase shoes to match gowns, with the bride-to-be trying on a number of different white models. We loved to serve those groups. The commissions were often healthy. Lots of trying on, walking around, and changing of their minds. Occasionally a customer was a "b-bac." Not being able to decide, she would say, "I'll be back," hence the term. That is when the "let no customer walk" policy was quickly activated.

In our opinion we were quite well paid: 6% on gross sales for the day, after the first $100.00 sold. Base pay was $.95 per hour. On a good eight-hour Saturday, the busiest day of the week, we would often take home $30.00 or more. We felt we had earned every penny, at least from a physical standpoint. Then there were the "kickers." This was a specialty shelf of shoes in the back room, which had not sold well. (I do not know why that name). If the salesman sold a customer one of these oldies, his result was a full 12% commission, not involving the first $100.00 up front. We completed a few of these sales each week. Of course, we were always trying.

Alas, my budding career as a shoe salesman came—literally—to a crashing halt, two weeks before school began again.

So, what happened? I was visiting a young lady named Pat Funk at her home on Santa Rosa Drive in mid-west Detroit. We were sitting on the cement steps, talking with her twelve-year-old brother, Jack. He said to me, "Hey Russ, don't try to lift the cement cap on top of that brick pillar, because it is too heavy for you." I lifted it. As I replaced it, the cap slipped and smashed the index finger on my left hand. No need to belabor my stupidity in taking Jack's challenge. But, a smashed index finger wrapped in several layers of gauze and tape cannot be used to fit shoes, or to twirl a shoehorn.

ଔ

HOUSE PAINTER: 1947

My first cousin, Carol Rodney Giesey (née Ellis), was married to Boyd Giesey. They lived on Shevlin Street in Hazel Park, a medium-sized suburb north of Detroit, Michigan. Their home was a one-and-a-half story bungalow. It was painted white. At that time, they had two children, Tom and Gretchen, ages eight and two.

Boyd's business, inline-welding at Progressive Welder, was booming.

He was the sales manager. He had little time for work around the house. So, before I had even begun to look for a summer job, he made me an offer: spend whatever time was necessary to paint the exterior of their home with two coats of Sherwin Williams best white lead-based paint. Plus, when that job was completed, wash the interior walls and ceilings in the living room, kitchen, and dining area, using Spic & Span cleaner.

The exterior painting was a blanket offer— $200.00. The interior pay rate was room by room, if and when I got to it. There were a couple of other provisos. I could live in the back bedroom on the second floor. I could use one of their autos in the evening. One of these vehicles was a brand new, 1947 Ford convertible with a tan top and full white sidewalls. Whenever the family was using this auto, I could use the blue Hudson 110—one of the fastest 0 to 60 vehicles in town. Not certain of the model year.

So, I said a quick "yes." My "boss" and I went to Pontiac to buy paint, a couple of wide brushes, and one for trimming windows. We also bought lots of turpentine for brush and hand cleaning at the end of each day. This turned out to be a summer job to remember. I slept late and followed the sun, thus always got to paint on the shady side of the house. Cousin Carol made me a full breakfast of my choice plus a nice lunch. Whenever Boyd got home, we had a full dinner. I did a lot of reading and resting. Also, a bit of dating: movies and even a dance on a tennis court in Stoppel Park, on the far west side of Detroit. As always, summer dates in those days often included much front or back porch sitting.

I painted the peak on one side of the house. The other side was obviously the same height. However, because of the side door plus a sod terrace leading up to the door, the placement of the ladder added circa five feet to the extension.

Boyd Giesey was six-feet, three-inches tall. He had been a star basketball player at Cass Technical High School, and then the same at Lawrence Institute of Technology. He was very athletic, and a scratch golfer at Red Run Golf Club. Boyd insisted that he, not I, was going to paint the peak on that "higher" side. His reasoning was that with his height, he would be standing four rungs below where I would need to stand to reach the peak. Not wanting to disappoint my cousin by marriage, I agreed to hold the ladder. I appreciated that offer.

The painting ended about four weeks after it began. Cleanup of spatters on windows, sidewalks, awnings took a bit of time. I went back home to Highland Park for a few days, then back to Shevlin Street for a week of wall washing. The summer was fast disappearing, making way for my returning to Highland Park Junior College. My average wage rate turned out to be $15.00 per room.

This work had not been as demanding as some previous summers. Plus, I moved entirely at my own pace. Having an auto at my disposal was really a monumental perk. On Labor Day, Boyd and Carol took me and my parents to his boss's house for a big cook out. His boss was Mr.

Gordon. He had a daughter named Judy. She was sixteen and had a girlfriend visiting from out of town. My boss (cousin Boyd) asked me if I would take the girls to the State Fair just down Woodward Avenue. I said, "I'm ready to go." He gave me five twenty-dollar bills, and said spend it all. We spent about sixty dollars, doing most everything there was to do there, including eating very well. Boyd would not take back the "change." I was rich. The girls loved the fair and riding around in that new convertible with the top down. Me too.

☙

SPOT WELDER: 1948

The 1948 Hudson Commodore four-door automobile was selling very well. It featured the first "step down" body design in automotive history. Seventy years later, we now step down into almost all of today's autos.

Because of the popularity of this new design, the Hudson plant located on the east side of Detroit, Michigan, was hiring temporary full-time men to work on several different production lines.

My friends Jim Snider, Dick Teneau, and I were college students, only available for summer work. This was not a deterrent to Hudson recruiters at that moment in time. They needed help right then. We applied as a threesome, since we had only one way to get to the plant. We had purchased a 1931 Model A Ford coupe with a rumble seat. We bought the auto solely for the purpose of being able to get to good paying factory jobs for the summer. We planned to sell it in the fall. The car had been put up for sale by a friend from our high school days, Jack McQuestion. The price was $25.00.

The auto needed a clutch and brakes, repairs that priced out at $75.00. We choked a bit on that, but chipped in and did it. Great investment. We drove it back and forth to the plant during the summer, until we got laid off, and then sold it in the fall for $150.00. We more than broke even, with "free" transportation to and from work, except for a little gas money at $.10 per gallon, plus a AAA three-month auto liability policy for three young men (I don't recall the cost). We were all insured, so each of us could drive every third day and be fully covered.

That driving every third day was interesting. We made out a schedule for the entire summer—five work days at a glance. Driver's seat #1—Passenger seat #2—Rumble seat #3. We all wanted to drive, and we all wanted to ride in the rumble seat, except on rainy days. We purchased a large light-weight tarpaulin for the rumble seat, and away we went to Conant and Six-Mile Road on Detroit's east side, the location of the Hudson Motor Car assembly plant.

Each of us was assigned to a different task at the plant. My assignment was as a spot welder with the battery frame group. As new employees, our hourly rate of pay was $1.48. Our shift was 8:00 A.M. to 5:00 P.M., with two paid breaks of fifteen minutes each, morning and afternoon. Lunch was a full hour, unpaid, to get us, in the words of the recruiter "rested up for the afternoon."

Training for my job entailed watching an experienced worker operate a spot-welding machine. Basically, this was two copper-tipped pincers coming together with a heavy wattage of electricity coursing into the tips. Two—or sometimes three—pieces of metal were properly placed between the tips before closing them down. The high voltage did the work of welding joints of various sizes and shapes.

Once learned, the task was really quite easy, and was fun for someone who had never been exposed to any real machinery. I had previously worked only with wood, including working with a wood lathe I had purchased from Sears because I wanted more practice than I could get in woodshop at school.

The parts of the battery cradles that I was welding were greasy. Heavy sparks from the welds flowed toward the floor. My Levis became oily, even though I had a clean pair each day, having scrubbed up one of the three pair I owned each night. Several times my Levis caught fire. Only then did I realize that other workers standing at spot welding machines had metal spark deflectors, which angled sparks away from their legs and feet. So, I asked my friendly foreman if I might have a deflector as well. His answer was a big surprise. He said, you probably need to ask the UAW union steward.

I had tried to avoid the union steward, because only being a summer employee, I did not want to join the union and have to pay the $6.00 per month dues. I had reasoned that $18.00 was more important in my pocket than in their treasury. However, my pants were being burned, and my flesh might be next. So, I succumbed, and approached the union steward. He could not have been nicer, or more understanding. He was also straightforward. He said, "the maintenance department will have a proper spark guard here before your shift begins tomorrow." I said, "Thank you—thank you." He continued, "maybe in appreciation you would slow down your battery cradle production numbers just a tad." At that moment, I had no idea what a tad was, but I got a spark guard, and I also got his message. I slowed down a little (which turned out to be a tad), and got through the summer at the Hudson Motor Car company with no problems. The steward never mentioned anything about my joining the union, and often nodded his approval in my direction as he passed by.

It had been the plan of our little carpool group to work until the last working day of August. That plan was cut short by the workers at the Continental Motors, Inc., plant in Muskegon, Michigan, who manufactured engines for Hudson Commodore automobiles. They went on strike in mid-July. Our Conant Avenue assembly plant had only a few days' supply of engines on hand. We all received layoff notices.

The money had been good. We had even been given a raise of $.05 per hour to $1.53. The experiences, we agreed, had been worthwhile. Jim went back to Wayne University early (later named Wayne State University) to work gratis in the medical research lab. Dick likewise went back early, to Washington University in St Louis to perfect his on-mike radio technique. I stayed home and prepared to move to Michigan State College (later University). I had enrolled as a junior in the School of Business & Public Service (later renamed Business Administration). My freshman and sophomore years had been at Highland Park Junior College, later renamed Highland Park Community College. Now defunct.

CB

SPRAY PAINTER: 1949

In the spring of 1949, the Cadillac Plating Company placed a "help wanted" ad in the *Detroit News*. I answered in person, as dictated in the ad. To get to the factory I took a Six-Mile Road bus west to Myers Avenue and then walked approximately one-half mile south to the factory. Any job I took had to have public transportation available. I was away at college, living in East Lansing, and had gone home to Highland Park for spring break. That is when I applied for this summer job.

I met the plating supervisor whose name is best forgotten. We had a tour of the operation, including watching their sole product, Chevrolet bumper guards, being chrome plated. At that time, the plating was done by dipping each piece into deep vats of first copper, then nickel, then chrome. Men with big shoulders and biceps stood on wooden platforms above these vats of liquid metal, submersing a rubber-covered rack of four raw metal guards into each vat in proper sequence, to build up to chrome. The length of time for each dip was set on a timer. The men wore rubber suits plus rubber aprons. A very archaic method of plating by today's standards.

The inside of the bumper was coated with a waxy material so it did not get plated. Somehow this was then washed off when the plating procedure was complete. When all of these steps were accomplished, the four bumper guards were moved on a wheeled rack into a shed-like room, to have the inside of the bumper spray-painted with silver lacquer. The painter wore a heavy-duty mask to filter out the odor and toxic fumes. The paint room was fitted with two large exhaust fans. Overalls were furnished, along with matching headgear. I agreed to become a painter-of-bumpers—Monday through Friday, 8:30 A.M. to 5:00 P.M., with a paid fifteen-minute break, morning and afternoon, plus a half hour for lunch. Hourly rate $1.75. This was a summer job, to fill in for regular employees taking vacations. I started painting on June 10th, the day after I arrived home from college.

This was a miserable job from day one. It was in a one-story flat-roof building. Many large fans blew around hot humid air. No air conditioning. (Not much anywhere in those days). No matter; even with that heavy-duty mask to filter the toxic odor of silver lacquer, and exhaust fans running at top speed, the smell still got through to your nose, clothes under the overalls, and into your hair. Yet I kept painting, and getting paid circa $70.00 every week. This was quite a good amount. To put it in perspective, tuition at the Michigan State College of Business was $45.00 for fifteen trimester credits—$135.00 total tuition for the school year.

On July 29, 1949, my maternal grandmother, Harriet May Stearns (née Jeffords) died. She had been ailing for some time. She was in a nursing home on Kerby Street, just north of midtown Detroit. Not many facilities of this type were available in those days.

Grandma was to be buried in her home town of Jamestown, New York, next to her husband Frank Marshall Stearns (1882–1917) and close to her parents' graves. Her casket would travel there via the Michigan Central Railroad freight line. Her family—two daughters and their families, including me—would drive to Jamestown separately.

I knocked on my boss's door. He waved me in. I had not been in the office since he had interviewed and hired me. I told him my sad story, and that I would need to be travelling

Friday through Tuesday, and come back to work on Wednesday.

I do not know what I expected, as this was a first for me. His response was: "You guys have too goddamn many grandmothers and grandfathers."

I don't think I said anything, just went back to work. That was Thursday.

The travel, the funeral service, and the interment ended as planned. We got home Tuesday afternoon.

I told my parents that I was not going to work for Great Lakes Plating Company anymore. My Dad said, "Did you tell your boss?" I said, "No—and I am not going to." He said, "You must." I said, "I won't." He said, "Did something happen?" I told my story. He said, "I agree." When my former boss called around noon to ask, "Where in hell are you?" I said, "I don't work there anymore," and hung up. That was the first and last time I ever did anything like that, because it was the only time I ever felt treated with disrespect. My grandmother had always been very important to me. Still, in all honesty, I probably would have gone back if it had not been for the toxic odor of that silver lacquer.

Interestingly enough, the next week I received a check for the three days I had worked before leaving for Grandma's funeral. I had a slight twinge of guilt, having left my boss in the lurch with no one to work the paint booth.

I have sometimes thought that Grandma Stearns died to save me. Those paint fumes, mixed with my seasonal allergies, were for sure not serving me well as I sprayed silver lacquer eight hours a day.

However, all was not lost. I already had a job working for the Michigan State College bookstore. I returned to East Lansing ten days before the start of classes, and went to work.

☙

BOOKSTORE CLERK: 1949

The bookstore at Michigan State College was located in the College Union.

As the school year was ending in the spring of 1949, there was a placard, on an easel, just inside the bookstore door. The purpose was to advertise for people to work for the bookstore for ten days prior to the beginning of fall term. I met the bookstore manager, Mr. Miller, and we struck a deal. My work would not be in the bookstore, but rather in the basement of the college auditorium. I would need to be on campus, ready to work, ten days before classes began.

In this enormous basement room were set many long tables, on which were many boxes of eighty-eight-column IBM cards. Each card represented a textbook title. Every required text, for all courses being offered that term in every department, would be represented via a punched card. This setup was for United States military veterans or active duty personnel only. Once officially enrolled in the college, and with proper ID, veterans visited this room to stand in line at each book station. A pre-punched and printed

IBM card for each book on his or her class list would be pulled and placed in an Official MSC envelope. All books were paid for by the U.S. Government. With these cards in hand, books could be picked up at the college bookstore in the Union.

My job was two-fold. First, using IBM equipment, I had to be certain sufficient keypunched cards were continuously available, for every book, at each departmental station where cards were being handed out. Second, I had to supervise the "floor," solving any situation involving the thirty-five female clerks or the hundreds of veterans seeking book cards.

I worked 140 hours during those fourteen days. Met many very charming young women workers who became friendly coeds living in all areas off and on the campus. My total income was $140.00. Total contacts with young women were almost unlimited.

ଔ

YMCA COUNSELOR: 1950

Summer jobs for college students were hard to find in 1950. However, as a full-rate member of the Highland Park, Michigan, YMCA, I found out about a job opening in the boys' department. The job was as a summer boys' work counselor. What a great job it turned out to be.

A boy's membership entitled him to use what was referred to as "front room facilities": two pool tables, two ping pong tables, wood-working shop, and even though it was really in the back room, the swimming pool. The gym was not a part of this membership. It did, however, include a variety of out-of-building activities.

Next to the front lobby was a lunchroom with tables and comfortable chairs for the lads' use, whether lunch was from home in a brown bag, purchased on site, or from the S&C trolley-car restaurant next door.

My job was to teach pool (billards) and ping pong; supervise swims, twice daily on hot days; and guide the building of scale-model wooden sailboats. One baseball game was scheduled, to see the Detroit Tigers at then-Briggs Stadium. We were transported via Greyhound bus to and from the stadium. Supervising this and other field trips was a serious part of my summer job responsibility.

A summer-long project for boys who wanted to participate was building a scale-model wooden sailboat. These craft would then participate in a boat race the Monday before Labor Day. The site for the race was a pond built just for this purpose at the Fisher YMCA, located on West Grand Blvd. (now abandoned). This competition was serious business for young boat builders. A silver-plated travelling cup was the prize. It traveled back and forth. My first year it travelled to Fisher, as their boat team won. My second summer working at the Highland Park "Y," we won it back. I have always wondered how many more years that tradition continued.

There were unlockable lockers for the lads to use on a daily basis for coats and lunches. These were emptied daily to avoid any leftover lunches, especially those containing egg salad sandwiches, which seemed to be a favorite to bring and then not eat.

This Northern YMCA was originally built with a major donation by Henry Ford. His original Model T plant was located about two miles north of the "Y," also on Woodward Avenue. The YMCA building was a four-story structure with sleeping rooms on the top floor. These were rented by the day or week, to men who were usually new to the city or country and just getting started on new jobs, often in local auto plants.

In addition, directly across the side street (Winona) was a duplicate building housing the YWCA, also part of Henry Ford's largesse. The only noticeable difference between the two programs was that the YWCA had Saturday night dances, and the YMCA did not. We never had any problem finding our way across the side street for those dances, called sock-hops.

Mickey McLaughlin was the Director of the YMCA—both the men's and boy's divisions. Bill Zophy and Lyle Box were his assistants. I reported to whichever one was on duty any particular day. They were both recent college graduates. They also had completed a YMCA post-graduate training program, funded and conducted by the organization. They were excellent men, both of whom felt fulfilled in their work, but not in their level of compensation.

As a summer employee, I was OK with the pay rate of $1.95 per hour. I lost track of Bill and Lyle over the years. However, my guess is that even though educated to be YMCA career employees, and very dedicated to the program, they both ended up in other careers.

☙

BUSBOY: 1950

After two years living in Mason-Abbot dormitory, on the campus of Michigan State College, I decided to join five friends and move into an off-campus house. The house was owned by Jim and Fifi McWilliams. Jim was a recently discharged veteran, and a friend of one of my five friends. He was enrolled in the business school, having had two years of college before being drafted.

Jim and Fifi had purchased a house at 511 Ann Street, one block off Grand River—the main street immediately to the north of campus. There were three bedrooms up, and one down. My room-mate-to-be was Bill Lanphar, from Romeo, Michigan. The three upstairs bedrooms had bunk beds. I took the top bunk.

The other two bedrooms were occupied by Ray Simescu and Paul Kelly—both hotel administration majors—and by Chuck Sumner and Lenny (last name not remembered). It was never clear if either of them ever matriculated. The rest of the deal included one bathroom on the second floor, one shower in the basement, and one telephone in the upstairs hallway for local and incoming calls only. It was a fun place to be. Each room had two desks and one wastebasket.

We all had use of the kitchen on Friday night plus all day Saturday and Sunday. That worked out quite well. Bill and Ray had convinced me to work with them as a busboy at the Alpha Gamma Delta sorority house, located just one block away. This turned out to be the best job of my lifetime.

Our remuneration as busboys was the opportunity to eat twenty-one meals each week in the basement kitchen. We had to arrange our class schedules to be at the sorority house from 11:30 A.M. until 1:00 P.M. for lunch, and from 5:30 P.M. until 7:00 P.M. for dinner. Lunch was not served on Saturday. Dinner was served at noon on Sunday, but no supper. Hence, we worked twelve meals per week. You are wondering about breakfast. The women living in the house were on their own for breakfast. My two housemates and I usually arrived in the kitchen around 7:00 A.M. every day. Coffee, juice, cereal, and sweet rolls, the same fare as the sorority sisters had, were available to us every day.

What made this job so demanding were those early morning breakfasts. We had to put up with eating breakfast with thirty-five women, eighteen to twenty-three years of age, often scantily clad in filmy pajamas or short night shirts. Difficult work, but as we forever opined, "someone has to do it."

This job allowed me to minimize my out-of-pocket expenditures. Room rent in the McWilliams home was $7.00 per person per week. Meals were now available free in the Alpha Gamma Delta kitchen. So, the dollars allotted to me by my parents allowed me to always have funds available for fun stuff. For that reason—and for another reason detailed below—I have forever considered this job the best of all worlds.

As busboys we were on call, after the women had been served, to answer the tinkling of a little bell located with the sorority sister sitting at the head of the table for that meal. Being at the head of the table rotated, thus teaching each woman to be a proper hostess.

My first night on the job, I was "selected" to answer all bells. I did. The first ringing was from a table where my friend Gill Eveland's wife Mitzi Eveland (née Dickens) was sitting. At the time, Gill was a prisoner of war in North Korea. Mitzi had been granted special permission from Alpha Gamma Delta international headquarters to live in the house, as married women were usually not allowed to do so.

Lou Bowen, the hostess at Mitzi's table, had rung the bell. Lou announced that Mitzi would like to have another helping of mashed potatoes. I made some offhand remark like "the next time I write Gill, I will mention you are eating well." I brought Mitzi more mashed potatoes. When I returned to the kitchen, I asked my roommate Bill, "Who is the little blond in the white sweater sitting on Mitzi Eveland's right?" His answer was three-fold; 1. Ginny Bristol from Battle Creek. 2. Mitzi's roommate. 3. Don't bother going there, she does not go out with anyone; she is pinned to Johnny LaParl—a childhood sweetheart from her home town.

The next afternoon, I called the Alpha Gamma Delta house general telephone number and asked for Ginny Bristol. She came to the phone. I explained that I was the new busboy who had brought Mitzi more mashed potatoes. She answered, "Oh yes, I remember." I said, "Would you like to walk up the hill to Shay's drug store for a cup of coffee? It is going to be a crisp, clear fall evening." She answered, "That would be nice." We walked—sipped slowly—talked. Ginny wore a mid-green corduroy suit. On the way down the hill, I said, "Someday you and I will be married." She did not say anything. The next Saturday, I called and asked her to join my roommate Bill and me in the basement of the house we lived in, to help us pluck a pheasant we had shot that afternoon from his new bronze-colored Ford convertible. She said, "I guess so." She helped us. Bill was amazed. It took a bit of doing, but over time, hometown Johnny became history.

☙

BOOKSTORE ASSISTANT SUPERVISOR: 1951

The job at the bookstore involved three registrations each year, since Michigan State was on a trimester in those days. That meant I worked three registrations in the 1949–1950 school year, plus another three during the 1950–1951 school year. The difference between the winter of '50 and spring of '51 registrations was that by then I had met my future wife Ginny, and had hired her—along with several of her sorority sisters—to work the IBM card files in the auditorium's lower level. This was the one and only time, during the entire time I have known Ginny, that she ever "reported" to me.

That second school year I worked for Mr. Miller, he put me in complete charge of the veterans book activity. This allowed him to run the bookstore.

I recruited, interviewed, selected, hired, trained, motivated, and supervised all clerks, plus an IBM punch-card operator. I worked many more hours at each of the three registrations, and at a 50% higher rate. Total income for each fourteen-day stint was $290.00.

Of course, the *biggest* payoff was being near Ginny. Of all those thirty-five clerks, she required the most training—very close supervision. And I was a hero in her Alpha Gamma Delta sorority house, for employing so many of her sorority sisters.

This job, which began in 1949 and carried over into 1950 and 1951, was a bit different in those last two years: it was my first time in management. The work was much more interesting and fulfilling (and far less toxic) than spray painting the inside of Chevrolet bumper guards.

In the summer of 1951, I was asked to return to the "Y," and I did. It was another great summer working with those enthusiastic boys. Plus, I was able to leave a bit early on Friday afternoons to catch the 4:30 P.M. Michigan Central train to Battle Creek to visit Ginny for the weekend. She was working the night shift at the Kellogg's cereal factory. Her job was to sit atop a high stool and pop a toy into each cereal box as they sped by on the conveyor line below. Shifts were six hours, and the line never shut down because they never turned off the ovens.

The Friday after Labor Day, 1951, I left the "Y" for the last time, to prepare for induction into the U.S. Army. I had received that dreaded, standard letter: "Greetings from your friends and neighbors. You have been selected by your local draft board for military service." That usually meant Army, as Navy, Marines, Air Force, and Coast Guard recruiting requirements were being filled via volunteer enlistments.

It was possible to receive an educational deferment to go to graduate school. It meant taking a test, and passing with a 75% or better score. Then you could file a plan for continuing your education. You could receive a year-by-year deferment, assuming you maintained passing grades. I took the test and qualified. Grade percentage unknown.

For a number of complex reasons, I decided to apply for Mortuary Science school at Wayne State University. I was accepted and enrolled, and began classes in early August. The first week was orientation. The second week we began the most difficult course—"Gross Human Anatomy." The huge laboratory housed an unremembered number of life-sized metal tubs filled with formaldehyde, and one cadaver per tub.

All specimens were indigents from the streets of Chicago. Each cadaver was on a metal platform, which was raised out of the preserving liquid by two class members—one at each end of the tub (vat)—pushing down on a crossbar handle. We began the six-week class, three hours per day, dissecting upper and lower back muscles. Four students to each cadaver. This experience was initially quite unnerving.

Much dissecting took place. In the second week of class, I became ill. Fever, chills, weakness in my limbs. I attributed it to the formaldehyde fumes, and although I no longer felt bothered at dissecting a human body, I thought this might also have something to do with my being unwell. I arranged an appointment with our family physician, Louis Gariepy, M.D. He diagnosed my condition as a virus. He said that it would take me from three to five weeks to recover. I was relieved to know that I was at least tolerating the rigors of Gross Human Anatomy. I also knew that it would be impossible to catch up with that class (eight credits) plus the other eight credits which had also begun. However, I could reschedule for winter term and still keep my advanced education deferment.

Ginny and I were engaged. She was very interested in getting married before I left for the Army; for me, that was not an option. Friends who had been in service told me that the most unhappy servicemen were those who had married just before induction. I faced a tough decision: get a temporary job until the new semester began in January and return to college, or ask for immediate induction. I reluctantly chose the latter, and was inducted on October 16, 1951.

Except for a tiny variance, I should already have left for the Naval Station at Great Lakes, in north Chicago, to attend officer training. This was because my roommate at Michigan State, Bill Lanphar, had told me about a program for college graduates to become Naval officers. His father was a retired Naval Commander, and still active in the reserve. With Bill's help, I got in contact with the 12th Naval District recruiter, located in the Lafayette building in downtown Detroit. I was able to set up an appointment to take a qualifying exam, which I did. It was scored within an hour. During that wait I partook of a Lafayette Coney Island hotdog, in that famous restaurant on the ground floor of the building where the test was administered.

Back to the Navy recruiting office, to receive results of the test. The Officer who had given the test sat across the desk and smiled. I thought I had passed. I had, sort of. However, not high enough. The cutoff score that day to receive an offer for the Naval Officer training program was 83. I had an 82. But, as he said, not to worry. Within a month, I would be awarded an opportunity at Great Lakes. My score was excellent. However, I had just missed that day's cutoff. The opportunity never materialized because the United States Army already had their hooks into me. Neither Commander Lanphar nor a friend of my dad's who was also a retired Navy Commander was able to break that draft board's hold. I did become a member of the United States armed forces, but the Army, instead of the Navy.

08

UNITED STATES ARMY

INFANTRY TRAINEE: 1951

Very early on the morning of October 16, 1951, my dad and mom drove me from our home in Highland Park to Fort Wayne at the foot of Livernois Avenue in Detroit, Michigan. I bid them adieu. This old fort (built in 1842) was now the staging area for all Army recruits and draftees from southeast Michigan. I was one of them. It was a very historical setting. I had graduated from Michigan State College in June.

I joined the mass of male humanity heading for the General Headquarters building, as we had been advised to do by letter. We arrived and were sorted into groups of, I think, twenty-five. We were herded into straight lines, just in back of a wide stripe of yellow chalk drawn on the cement floor. We stood in back of this chalk line and repeated a pledge to defend the USA, as read aloud by a 2nd Lieutenant (one gold bar on each shoulder). We were then advised that, once we had "voluntarily" stepped over that yellow line, we would be in the United States Army. Everyone in my line "stepped."

Then there was a bit of paperwork to be completed by a battery of clerks. The first rumor, of the *one million* rumors experienced while I was in the Army, was that we were going by rail to Fort Custer, just outside of Battle Creek, for processing. I hoped that rumor would come true, as, Ginny, my future wife, lived in that west Michigan town. Amazingly, this rumor was accurate.

We were bused to the Michigan Central Depot, just up Fort Street from Fort Wayne. We boarded the train, arriving in Battle Creek about supper time. We were bused to a row of barracks that would be our home for the next two weeks. We were fed in a mess hall, the first government meal of many.

Our work was: 1. To be tested, to determine our mental agility to become officers, commissioned or non-commissioned. 2. To complete lots more paperwork. 3. To receive "dog tags," which we were ordered to wear "at all times until we were discharged from the Army." They were strung on a bead-like metal chain, stamped with our name, rank, and serial number. If you died, in or out of combat, one tag went to headquarters, to be used as a printing plate from which to print your death notice; the other tag would be attached to your dead body for transport. Information of this sort was, of course, heartening to learn about on my second day in service. Plus, even at that early date we were told that our name, rank, and serial number, as embossed on our name tags, were the only information we should give if we were ever captured by an enemy. That had been agreed to at the Geneva Convention, to which the United States had subscribed long ago.

So, for two weeks we got processed and worked as KP's (Kitchen Police). Peeled a ton of potatoes, washed dishes, scrubbed pans, swept and wet-scrubbed mess hall floors until they were bleached almost white. We went on "police call" several times each day (lined up and walked the entire area, picking up cigarette butts, candy wrappers, and even little stones above a certain size). We washed the barrack's windows, inside and out, with a small bucket of water, a roll of toilet paper, and lots of elbow grease. All of this work would be duplicated at every military installation to which I was ever assigned. Then we washed those clean windows again.

Ginny came home from college on the two weekends I was at Fort Custer. My parents visited the last Sunday I was there (October 24, 1951). I had a four-hour pass. The four of us went to the *original* Bill Knapp's for dinner. That would happen again 27 months later, on January 22, 1954, when my parents and I had dinner there the night before Ginny and I were married. Ginny did not join us on that occasion. She and her dad had had dinner at that first restaurant in an eventual chain the day it had opened in Battle Creek.

Rumors were flying as to where we would go for our sixteen-weeks of infantry basic training: Camp Breckenridge, Kentucky, and Schofield Barracks at Fort Shafter, Hawaii, were both in the mix. These surmises were both correct.

I was the number two alternate for basic in the Islands. On the train siding, at 4:00 A.M., the Breckenridge group was loading. The numbers one, two, and three Hawaii alternates were waiting. Number one alternate was called out, to wait for a flight to San Francisco the next day, and then to catch a troopship to Hawaii. My number, two, did not get called, so I also boarded the train for Kentucky. (Note: The Hawaii group completed basic training and went directly to Korea, without a leave of absence. They paid quite a price for those beautiful surroundings during their four months of basic training.)

Camp Breckenridge was home to the "Screaming Eagles" 101st Airborne Division, a unit with a great tradition from WWII at the Normandy beachhead. It was now converted to a basic training division in the States. Even though we were not going to train to be jumpers, we wore that American eagle patch with pride.

I was assigned to the 4th Platoon—"G" Company (George). There were, of course, Battalion and Regimental designations as well. These did not mean anything to me. I was only interested in our Company's First Sergeant. He was Master Sergeant Churchill.

"Sarge" was a large man. He turned out to be the epitome of what a soldier could and should be. That first morning, and every morning for the next four months, the "barracks" (that was all of us) fell out at 5:00 A.M. for first inspection. Uniforms were pressed, hair cut short, boots polished, face shaved. I had carefully shaved. Standing close in front of me was my new leader. He said, "Did you shave, soldier?" "Yes sir." "Then tomorrow stand closer to your razor." That brief exchange, and numerous others like it, would mark everyone's entire time in the military. In time I would be asking that—and similar questions—of others. BTW—Master Sergeant

Churchill was what we called in those days a "negro," and the best non-commissioned officer I ever encountered. The southern boys in Company "G" respected this man with a reverence seldom given to any human being. They frequently said that they would follow him anywhere. Me, too.

Christmas was coming. We had completed approximately one-half of our sixteen-week basic training. The camp bulletin board announced that there would be five-day passes over Christmas, from December 23 through December 27; report back for reveille at 0600 hours, on the 28th. This offer was for troops with no demerits on their record during the past three months.

There were four of us from the Detroit area in the 4th platoon. The only name I remember was Glenn. He was from Dearborn. He was tall, blond, and slightly stoop-shouldered. He had run the mile for the Fordson high school track team. Our team of four decided we would try to get home for Christmas, even though we had only been away from home for about eleven weeks.

We visited the PX where we were able to purchase train tickets to Detroit.

The route was through Chicago, arriving at the Michigan Central Depot on the southwest side of the city. We bought our roundtrip tickets. Price not remembered. Leaving from the St. Louis terminal at 6:00 P.M. December 22, arriving Detroit 8:00 A.M. December 23. A change of trains in Chicago.

We were able to leave Camp at noon on December 22nd. Our route was: walk to the main gate (Camp Breckenridge). Hail a taxi to Morgantown, Kentucky, about two miles away. Take a local bus to the Evansville, Indiana, Greyhound bus station. Take a bus (we already had tickets, and the schedule matched our timing) to St. Louis. Timing went to perfection. We arrived in St. Louis. It was only a brief taxi ride to the gigantic train station. That is where our well-laid plans fell apart.

Posted above the ramp to the track level was a notice that read: "Train No. (our number) 12-hour delay. See ticket agent for more information." We gathered at the ticket agents' wire-protected window. A "track tear-up" a couple hundred miles west had prevented our train from reaching St. Louis. All would be back in order by noon the next day. Not good for GI's with only a few hours at home, and many of those going up in smoke.

Glenn of Dearborn came to our rescue. "Let's take a taxicab." Disbelief was registered by his three buddies—us. Glenn continued, "We all have a pocket full of money, so why not spend it." He was not asking a question. Even though our pay was only $65.00 per month, we did not have many places to spend it, other than on 3.2 (near) beer at the PX, along with a few bags of pretzels.

We approached the line of taxi cabs outside the station. We explained what we would like to do to several drivers in the line. Responses were different, all meaning the same thing. "No way." "You are out of your minds." "Wait for the noon train," and more. However, when we got near the end of the line, there was a cab which was not painted like all the others. It was a driver/owner whose name was Josh. He had a nice clean Chevrolet four-door. He was willing to listen. We asked him for a price. He hesitated, then responded $50.00 per man, plus we would buy all the gas and his food when we stopped to eat. Josh was going to end up with a net of $200.00. At that time in history when a new college graduate entered the workforce in a major corporation they were paid about $200.00 per month. Our knapsacks went in the trunk of Josh's taxicab and away we went.

We were on the road just shy of twelve and a half hours, 519 miles. This included two stops for gas and the latrine, plus a fairly lengthy layover for a large breakfast and rest period. The plan was to have Josh drop us off on the long looping driveway in front of the Dearborn Inn, in Dearborn, Michigan. We had all called home to fill the family in as to our ETA—8:00 A.M. EST. A few miles from Dearborn we told Josh to stop at a gas station so we could buy him a final tankful of gas to start his trip home. He was appreciative. We were more appreciative. When he had called his wife from St Louis, to inform her about the trip, we heard him tell her that he would be home by Christmas Eve day in time to go shopping for some great gifts for the kids.

We reached the Dearborn Inn oval driveway. Shook hands all around, especially with driver Josh. Promised to meet at the Michigan Central train depot at 8:00 A.M. on December 27th for the return trip to camp. All went as planned.

I looked down the line of cars on the driveway. Our family auto was there holding the family, Dad, Mom, and my someday-to-be wife, Ginny. The next four days sped by. The difficult trip had all been well worth it.

Back at the camp for the next eight weeks, we ran, marched, and did tons of calisthenics. We learned to disassemble, clean, oil, and reassemble our M-1 rifles (traditionally referred to as our "piece"). We ended up being able to do these functions in total darkness, and did. We spent endless hours on the shooting range, firing at distances of 100 to 500 yards. The targets were hauled down after so many rounds had been fired. Hits and misses were then recorded. Bullet holes were papered over with little stamp like stickers before the next round of shooting. Each shooter received a score depending on the number of hits in and around the bullseye. The hauling up and down of targets was done by each of us, on a rotating basis. The pits were dug-outs, behind and below the targets, which were pushed up and lowered as the shooting progressed. When a shooter missed the target area altogether, we got to wave a white flag on a long stick. The miss was called hitting "Maggie's drawers." That was the only good part of being in the pits, which that job definitely was. I qualified as a "sharpshooter," one notch below the top classification—"expert." I did not get the drawers. In those days we were not given headsets to protect our ears. Hence, the muzzle blast from the rifle subtly injured ears, left ear if you were right handed; right ear if you were left handed.

The most detested work encountered during basic training was that of "fire-guard." This entailed an entire night of keeping fires stoked in George Company's four barracks, plus—and this is the worst part—lighting the three wood-burning cook stoves in the mess hall, at 3:30 A.M., for the mess sergeant's arrival at 5:00 A.M. I was awful at getting these stoves burning to the cook's satisfaction, having only stood next to a wood-burning stove once in my life, and had never built a fire in one. As it would turn out, the worst chewing outs I received in my time in the Army would come from mess sergeants. However, when the chewing was over, they would grab hunks of wood, handfuls of newspapers and kindling, jam it all in the top of the stove, light it, and have a roaring blaze in a heartbeat. They all would give you that look, without a word "why in hell didn't you do that one-and-a-half hours ago—idiot?" Then they would laugh, and slap you on the back. They knew why—it was a very difficult chore, which they had learned over many, many years. It was amazing to me that in 1952, the United States Army was still using wood to cook food at a major training facility.

We learned to use our bayonet to kill the enemy in close quarters. There is a best way to withdraw the blade from the enemy's wounded or dead body, as on occasion it will get hung up in bone and gristle. Sergeant Churchill had been in combat in WWII, and recently in Korea. His job was to teach us how to stay alive in combat. He did an outstanding job of it.

Basic training was just that, *basic*, and we repeated all lessons over and over, a minimum of seven reps for most activities. However, our final exercise was only a onetime affair. We had practiced crawling on both our bellies and backs, with our M-1 rifles held above our heads or out in front of us, to always keep our pieces out of the dirt or mud. The final crawl was fifty feet, at night, under barbed wire strung taut three feet above the ground, with live "friendly support fire" from thirty-caliber air-cooled machine guns coming from the rear, purported to be three feet above our heads. This was quite an incentive to "keep your head down." A passing grade meant that you did that task well, and lived to tell about it. The rumor was that the machine guns being used were so old that the bullets coming out of the muzzles sometimes dipped lower than the three-foot aim. Quite comforting.

We had a now forgotten number of night training sessions. We were reminded frequently that darkness was our friend, because we could not be seen by the enemy. No mention was made that we also could not see the enemy. The points being made had to do with how not to be seen in the dark. For example, we were all sitting on a hillside in total darkness, when across the valley one of the instructors lit a cigarette. It was one mile away from our position and seemed to light up the entire valley. Then that same person smoked the cigarette. The burning tip gave away that precise location. We could easily have called in mortar fire. Noises while moving about in the dark sound many times louder than by day, as there are fewer other sounds and distractions, and our ears are able to hear more.

Bivouacs were quite frequent, working, then sleeping, in the open without benefit of a tent. Later we moved up to pup tents, learning to erect one in a short period of time, including trenching just outside the tent's edge for rain to run off, not onto, the tent's dirt floor.

That first bivouac was the most memorable for two reasons. First, it was the first. Second, as I laid down in an open area within a grove of trees, I felt something jab me through my sleeping bag. I rolled up my sack and investigated. Amazingly, there was a perfect pink flint arrowhead. That was to me an omen: the next two years would go well. I carefully stored this new treasure in my backpack, for mailing to Ginny as soon as possible.

Fast forward eleven years: our oldest son Eric is seven, in second grade. "Show and tell" time has arrived in school. We had a small collection of Indian arrowheads, several from Ginny's grandmother's farm, plus that pink beauty from the Kentucky woods. Eric selected that one. He got the facts straight, and off to school he goes with his show-and-tell arrowhead. He made his presentation. However, the pink flint arrowhead never made its way back to our little box of arrowheads. How, where, why, who was never discovered. It did not seem to matter; the good omen had already brought us a long, long way.

Were there other happenings during that sixteen weeks? Of course—too many to even begin to describe. There were times to call Ginny and my parents. Times to read in the dayroom, and to have a 3.2 beer or two at the PX (Post Exchange) where you could buy almost anything at reasonable prices.

We had two weekend leaves. On one of those I got a ride with a friend, George Yeckley, a fellow Michigan State grad from the dorm where I had lived on campus. George was from Louisville, Kentucky. We just happened to be in basic training together. He was in the 3rd Platoon of George Co. and owned an auto. One weekend my parents set out from Michigan to visit me. Their green 1952 Ford broke down in a small town outside Louisville. George's route home passed through that town, so he dropped me off at Dad and Mom's motel on Friday evening, and picked me up on the way back to camp on Sunday evening. A sad remembrance of that trip was that on the two-lane highway leading back to camp, we were passed by an auto going at breakneck speed. As that auto shot past and down the hill in front of us, it went out of control, into the left side ditch, then out and across the road into the right-side ditch.

We pulled up and got out, thinking we might be able to help. The police were there immediately, as they had been chasing this vehicle. They took over, assessing the condition of the three soldiers in what was left of the auto. The driver and the front right-side passenger were dead. The back-seat passenger was still alive. One of the policemen asked me for my olive drab, army-issue topcoat, to cover the one survivor, to "prevent shock." His two buddies were both going to be using their dog tags earlier than planned.

I handed it over. When I was being checked out to go to my next post (job) and had no topcoat in my inventory, the supply sergeant prepared a "Statement of Charges" (very common in the military) for one topcoat—$30.00. My monthly pay at that time was $75.00. Why the three soldiers in that destroyed auto were being chased by the authorities I never learned; nor did I learn the fate of the third victim.

☙

NON-COM LEADERSHIP TRAINEE: 1952

When I had taken that battery of tests at Fort Custer a few months earlier, I guess I passed, because I was offered a spot in Officer's Candidate School (OCS) at Fort Benning, Georgia. I accepted the opportunity. However, the next opening was a couple of months away, so I was automatically enrolled in an eight-week, non-commissioned officer (NCO) leadership school, still at Camp Breckenridge. Having finished infantry basic training, I was now a Pvt. E-1, at $95.00 per month. It was a $20.00 per month increase.

Leadership School was on the other side of camp. I moved my gear to a barracks identical to the one I had lived in for the previous four months. One week later I began that new job: "learning to lead." I would no longer have to pull fire-guard duty.

The eight-week non-com (NCO) leadership course only lasted two weeks for me. Orders were cut and posted for my attendance at Officer Candidate School (OCS) — Fort Benning, Georgia. The only thing I remember from those two weeks was a chant we were taught to use when taking troops on long distance runs. The in-charge cadre member was to start the chant. It was said the troops enjoyed joining in the vocalizing. The purpose was to take their minds off the torture of the distance. It went like this: "left — right — left right — left my wife and twenty-four kids on the brink of starvation and thought I was right — left — right — left." There were many other such chants, and even many more verses to this one, which I cannot recall.

The good news for me was, I received a promotion to Corporal (CPL) even though I did not complete the eight weeks; plus, a ten-day leave. I went home to Highland Park.

ଔ

OFFICER CANDIDATE: 1952

It was a very long Greyhound bus ride from Highland Park, Michigan, to Columbus, Georgia, the nearest city to Fort Benning's Officer Candidate School (OCS). However, from there, the Army took over. A camp bus picked up all candidate arrivals, taking us to the proper building on this immense U.S. Government military reservation, where we would train to become infantry officers in the Army of the United States of America.

Checking in and being assigned to a particular training unit was efficient.

Dinner had been prepared. We "strolled" over to the mess hall to partake. This would be the last time we would stroll there—or anywhere else—for the balance of our stay in OCS. We jogged, ran, or double-timed everywhere on the base whenever we went as a group, and we were usually in one.

Our barracks was a duplicate of all others with which I had become familiar. On the second (top) floor, at one end of the building, was a "squad room." This room housed cadre for the barracks. The rank of those persons depended on a variety of criteria. In basic training, they were usually corporals; in non-com officer leadership school, usually sergeants 1st Class. In OCS, usually 2nd lieutenants, or at least master sergeants. One of these leaders was almost always in residence. In their words to "help us," or better yet "to show us how to help ourselves."

OCS was a capsule repeat of Basic and Leadership Training. The major difference was intensity. We ran faster, farther, and more often. We "fell out" of the barracks for inspections with greater purpose, and pace, or at least it seemed that way. We did more pushups, and more often, plus other types of exercise: sit ups, full knee bends, running in place, and other conditioners which our drill sergeant seemed to make up as he went along. We anticipated that we would do the "barbed wire—machine gun fire" drill more than once. Wrong; we did it only once. We marched more often in formation, especially during reviews of the troops by various levels of command.

There was one serious addition to OCS—the compass. We had classroom work with maps and compasses. We had daylight exercises in the field, locating rallying points and "enemy positions." It was that multitude of night work, with the maps and compasses, which was the most difficult. This vast military reservation had innumerable empty silos. We spent several midnights locating one or more of these landmarks, working only with coordinates. Our instructor was a captain. He taught with aplomb, wit, and incredible knowledge. He made it look easy. It wasn't. No one caught on fast. In time we all got it right, but not without becoming lost, confused, and frustrated, more than once.

So, what else was different? More classroom work in a variety of other arenas, materials conservation, ammunition, clothing, food, health issues in the field, vehicle maintenance, camouflage, and pup tent assembly. Strategy was explained more than really being taught. Strategy came down from above. Infantry 2nd lieutenants carried it out, hopefully to perfection.

In the barracks, classrooms, field exercises, parades, bivouacs, forced marches, long runs, inspections, and even in the mess hall, the way this intense training was structured and conducted instilled an amazing camaraderie in almost every participant. The few candidates who just did not fit into this intense discipline disappeared, as if by magic. Occasionally someone would be missing from morning formation. No one knew where he was. No one dared ask.

The weeks sped by. Graduation and acceptance of a commission as a 2nd lieutenant, Infantry was looming. I was in full-blown decision mode. Even after weeks of enduring the most demanding physical and mental challenges of my life, I was considering resigning in week twenty-one—seven days before our graduation day. Below is a mockup of the decision matrix I used to make this life-changing decision.

Mark Twain wrote of "decision-making" in simple terms. He divided a piece of paper into halves, by drawing a line down the middle. On one side he wrote "PRO;" on the other side he wrote "CON." I employed his method and the answer came out as stated below.

PRO: I would be a Commissioned Officer, like my cousin Jack. No other member of our family had achieved that distinction.

CON: I would have to sign up for three more years of service. I had already been in the Army for ten months of the two years I had been drafted to serve.

PRO: I would receive a decent salary, with good healthcare benefits.

CON: It would delay the career I hoped to have in the business world, for at least three years.

PRO: Ginny and I could get married, and if I were stationed in the USA, she could join me. We could live in officer housing on the base or off base.

CON: Officer housing, I had seen, was minimal; housing near the bases I had seen was less than that and expensive. Plus, if Ginny joined me, she would need to give up her new teaching position.

PRO: Once commissioned, there was a fifty-fifty chance of going to Europe (EUCOM) for a first assignment.

CON: If you resigned, the Army felt betrayed. The big red FECOM ink stamp would be applied to your records. That meant Far East Command (code words for KOREA).

PRO: Possibility of a career in the Military.

CON: Moving often, especially if with children, would be involved and did not appeal to me, nor to Ginny. Plus, my degree was in Business.

With Ginny's full support for either choice, I decided to resign. I visited the Battalion

Commander—a Major. He heard me out. He said, "Are you certain this is what you want?" I said "yes." He picked up a large rubber stamp, smashed it down on a red-ink pad, and slammed it down on the front of my record folder. He grunted "Dissss—missed." I saluted, turned smartly on my heel, and left. I was once again a combat infantryman.

ଔ

COMBAT INFANTRYMAN: 1952

The next two weeks I stayed at Fort Benning, working with an outside contractor who had been hired by the Army to demolish condemned barracks. Then had a ten-day furlough, much enjoyed in Michigan with Ginny, friends, and family. I had been given a train ticket from Detroit, Michigan, to San Francisco, California, with a reporting date and time to arrive at Camp Stoneman near San Francisco.

My ten-day leave was bittersweet. When it ended, I knew I was off to a new job as a combat infantryman in a combat zone. This occupation was known by most everyone to be a very challenging task and a dangerous one.

I was able to redeem the train ticket for cash. I added a few dollars and bought a plane ticket on an American Airlines DC-3 prop. The flight was bumpy, especially over the Rockies. It was my first time in a commercial aircraft. When the stewardess put a pillow on my lap, I wondered what was next. It was only for a dinner tray. The pillow was meant to cushion the tray of food being eaten, should an air-pocket drop occur.

Even then it was said that some morsels—or more—occasionally hit the ceiling. Mine didn't. The pillow worked.

Arrival in San Francisco was eventful. Cousin Jack and his wife Merry were at the airport to meet me. I spent the night at their home in Walnut Creek. They drove me to Camp Stoneman the next morning. Jack, having been an officer in WWII, had credentials to drive in and around military installations. Until I had a shipping-out date, I was usually free to come and go as I wished. My cousins took me to the original Trader Vic's restaurant, where we shared a Scorpion Bowl cocktail—Oh my, what a "trip" that was. We had breakfast at the Cliff House overlooking the Pacific Ocean. We sat next to famous singer Lilly Pons. We had seen her pink Cadillac, two pink poodles, and chauffeur in pink uniform outside the restaurant. We also ate fresh-caught Dungeness crab, purchased on Fisherman's Wharf outside of Joe DiMaggio's restaurant. The proprietor knew cousin Jack by name. He whacked two huge crabs to kill them. Jack prepared a massive crab salad which we consumed on their deck, overlooking an ocean inlet. We visited Golden Gate park, and the world famous aquarium. Sipped tea in the Japanese garden. Being wined and dined by my cousins was an unexpected bonus. Being driven around the San Fran area in their red Plymouth convertible was a wonderful send-off for a Korea-bound infantryman.

I was at Stoneman for ten days. We all received a number of shots. The worst was the yellow fever injection. Some men were affected to the point of falling flat on their faces. I didn't, but the smarting and a hot arm stayed with me for several days.

We all received a large duffle bag. Clothing for combat was packed tightly, including a helmet liner and a steel pot to wear on top of it. New orders appeared daily on the camp bulletin board. I did a check almost hourly. My orders were finally cut to ship out on the U.S.S. General Walker, a troop ship preparing to carry 4,490 troops and 270 officers to Korea, by way of Japan. Initial destination was Yokohama harbor.

I boarded. I did not get seasick. I was assigned as a fireman, and located in a forward area with many hundreds of feet of fire hose and nozzles. Duty was seven hours per day during the entire trip, circa eleven days. Navy food was great! Excitement in mid-Pacific, was when we exchanged movie reels with a sister ship bound for San Francisco. One of the movies was Doris Day in *Tea for Two*. I still enjoy hearing the music from that flick, with its reminder of the hope that a heart given away will be handled with care. We watched it twice at sea.

Other recreation, when not on duty, involved dice. There were not really any facilities to play cards, so shooting crap was the game of the day. I took the dice a few times during the long sea voyage. I got hot and the dollars mounted. Other times, I watched the shooter and made a few side bets. All in all, I came out with $900.00. The only way to send money home was via Postal Money Orders. I bought three totaling $750.00; $250 was the maximum face value.

I wrote to my parents, asking them to deposit $500.00 in my bank account, and to buy a new chair for their living room. They complied with my instructions. They visited Pioneer Furniture on East Grand Blvd. The chair they purchased with those dollars won in mid-Pacific was very nice. They used it in Highland Park, Royal Oak, and Redford. Today, sixty-five years later, upholstered in a different fabric, it resides with son Jeff and daughter-in-law Audrey in their lovely home on a mountainside in North Carolina, a memento from the Korean police action.

On board sleeping arrangements were hammocks, strung three high. Food was served continuously, three squares a day, via a never-ending cafeteria line. The standup tables were just above belt high, wide enough for your tray full of food. It was an amazing sight to see 400 troops standing at these long counter-like tables, enjoying the fare. Everyone had a scheduled time to eat, otherwise the 4,490 diners would never have gotten served. Officers had their own sit-down dining area.

After arriving in Yokohama harbor, we spent three days at Camp Drake in Tokyo. One evening while I was touring the city, the train stopped. The memory of the Japanese underground rail service will never leave me. Sliding doors opened for only a few seconds. Passengers scurried on or off. Doors slammed shut. The train was off and running. You had better move fast, or you would be waiting for the next train, or riding to the next stop.

Orders were cut for me to attend a two-week long Chemical, Biological, and Radiological (CBR) warfare school, at Sasebo, on Kyushu, the southernmost Japanese island. Getting there was by train along the entire length of the empire. We passed innumerable fishing villages and the eternally famous Mount Fuji, on Honshu, the middle island in the chain. At one crossroad stop, local Japanese women boarded the cars selling bottles of Seagram's 7 Crown whiskey. Many bottles were snatched up by the troops at fifteen American dollars per. The seals were unbroken. Surprise came with the first sip—sea water. We found out later that these folks spend hours with a diamond pointed tool hand drilling a tiny hole in the bottom of the bottle. When they reached the whiskey, the bottle was hung by a tether. It would drip for days into a vat. The real stuff was then rebottled and sold at incredibly high prices to fellow countrymen and women. Then the sea water was pushed into the bottle under pressure, leaving Seagram's official seal intact, with paraffin holding in the sea water—and then sold to gullible GI's on their way to the front lines.

The CBR school was located on a WWII Japanese air base. The buildings were still there, but the planes were gone. The most interesting leftovers were many hundreds of deteriorating fake trees, mounted on wooden pallets. During the war, these pallets had been pulled by tractors onto the runways, making the airbase look like an orchard from the air.

The two weeks went quickly. We learned to use different types of Geiger counters and to detect a variety of chemicals, using other chemical solutions, dyes, and by smell. Then we were taken to nearby woods and fields in protective suits with plastic viewing windows. We carried kits containing eye droppers and corked vials, to collect samples of water from leaves, creeks, pools, and puddles. These samples were returned to a makeshift lab in one of the hangers. Chemical, Biological, and Radiological samples had been placed in several locations for us to locate and collect. Our training was meant to demonstrate how to locate and detect these CBR weapons, if they were ever used by Chinese or North Korean enemies.

So, after sixteen weeks of Basic Training, two weeks of Non-Com Leadership Training, twenty-one weeks of OCS, and two weeks of CBR instruction, the time had come to go to a war deemed by Congress as a "police action." They never did declare war in Korea. It sure seemed like a war to me. Our CBR group boarded a small ship, and sailed across the Korea Straight to the city of Pusan in South Korea. This was my new job, Combat Infantryman, in a combat zone. It lasted eight months, from November 1952 to July 1953. It proved to be a most challenging experience. By comparison, Officer Candidate School, even the compass work, was a stroll in the park.

In Pusan, Korea (later officially renamed Busan), we were billeted in a supply depot. This massive compound was the staging area for all supplies that would soon be moving to the troops, as far north as the thirty-eighth parallel. Soon, I would be among those troops receiving these supplies. We had a full day of training on how to walk guard duty on the perimeter of the compound. This area covered approximately one square mile, enclosed by an eight-foot-high chain-link fence. Every 500 feet there was a floodlight shining outward toward the fields that surrounded the enclosure. Each light pole signified the beginning and ending of a guard post.

As we waited for a train north to the combat zone, we were assigned to guard duty patrolling these posts. Daytime was not a problem. After dark the coverage doubled, and that is what we were trained to do—effectively. Infiltration, even though the fence which included razor or barbed wire atop the chain links, was not uncommon. We were protecting every imaginable kind of supply. A few generic examples: foodstuffs, ammunition, vehicles, weapons up to and including M2—60mm mortars, and much, much more.

One full day of training taught us to intercept persons coming over, through, under, or around the fencing. Night guard duty included loaded weapons, with fixed bayonets; these to discourage anyone from jumping from the fence top onto a fixed, steel, pointed bayonet, held skyward. Question: who might try to breech security, and enter the compound? Answer: military personnel from both North and South Korea, AWOL Chinese soldiers, plus civilians of any sort. Every item in the compound was immediately usable by thieves, or saleable on the immense black market.

We took this guard duty very seriously. After that daylong indoctrination, we felt ready. "Sergeants of the Guard" were all combat veterans. Shifts were two hours on, and two hours off. When they came to wake you for your next shift, they spoke with stern authority. We were beginning to feel very much like we were in enemy territory, and we had better stay alert. In hindsight, that guard duty indoctrination was, for certain, part of a plan to get us believing we were in a war. This serious guard duty ended for me after just three nights, all without incident.

We were put aboard a rickety, coal-fired, steam-engine train, pulling four passenger cars full of troops. It headed north from Pusan. The roadbed was amazingly smooth. It was a long journey, just shy of halfway up the 680-mile Korean peninsula. This trainload of infantrymen was part of the total replacement effort for the 45th Infantry Division, Oklahoma National Guard. These troops had been on the line for a long time. General Clark Ruffner was Division Commander.

We passed 179th Regimental headquarters and reached the 2nd Battalion headquarters. Here we left the train for canvas-covered trucks. We also left our large canvas duffle bags, which contained non-combat gear. The supply sergeant promised to store them until we "hopefully" picked them up on the way back. My assigned vehicle was headed to the G-Company command post, at the base of a small mountain named "the Ice Cream Cone." This outpost was on the far-right flank of Heartbreak Ridge. More importantly, the mountain faced the Mung Dung Ni Valley. This locale had been the scene of a very bloody battle ten months before I arrived. We would be in what was now deemed a holding position. In the pages that follow, references to "mountain" or "hill" should be recognized as synonyms, in keeping with GI usage when they were in Korea in the 1950s.

I jumped from the rear of the truck, and was immediately greeted by Sgt. Jim Lagoe. Jim and I had been in basic training together at Breckenridge in Kentucky. He was from a small town in Michigan (Marion, near Mt. Pleasant), had graduated from Central Michigan University, and was drafted, soon after, just like I had been. He had seen my name on "Orders for the Day," and even knew my ETA.

We had spent some time together in the Camp Breckenridge base library, on Sunday afternoons, reading and palavering about a variety of issues. We also had quaffed a few 3.2 beers in the PX, on Saturday evenings. Running into a buddy at the base of a mountain in Korea was, in my opinion, a *miracle*. The next miracle was when he asked me if I could type. My Dad had encouraged me to take typing in high school (thirty-eight girls and me in the class). Then, when I "earned" a "D" grade, he strongly recommended that I repeat the course, which I did, for an "A." Thus, I was able to answer Jim's question with a decisive "yes." His MOS (Military Occupational Specialty) was company clerk. He was located in the command post at the bottom of the hill. It was a day to remember, Thanksgiving Day, 1952.

To rotate out of Korea required twelve points. Two points for each month in a combat zone, and one point for each month anywhere else on the peninsula. After four months in a combat zone, Jim had become G-Company clerk, moving to the rear with eight points. He was just completing his second month of being 1000 yards behind a combat zone. He needed two more points (2 months) to rotate. That would be circa January 15, 1953.

The next step was for me to get up the mountain into the trench line, and to my assigned bunker, called a "Hoochie." The primary meaning of that word is: "any barracks-like living accommodation; especially during the Korean police action."

Per Jim, I would soon be called to company headquarters for a one-on-one interview with Capt. Wendt—our Company Commander. If all went well, I would leave the hill on January 8th for a week of orientation with Company Clerk Lagoe. He would then be headed home. Jim owned a portable Royal typewriter, exactly like the one my Mother and I used back home. He had purchased it from his predecessor for $100.00. No pressure on me to buy it, except, in his words, "when you are doing the Morning Report longhand, each day, you will wish you had purchased the typewriter." I paid the asking price on the spot, $150.00, even before I had been approved for the job. Jim said that the 50% price increase was because his parents had sent two new typewriter ribbons, which he had not yet had to use. They were part of the package. *Jim was a true friend.* I still had a bunch of cash left over from those troopship crap games, when I had been on a roll. Money was not a problem.

We parted. I headed up the mountain. We were being led by G-Company Executive Officer First Lieutenant Broderick. About two-thirds of the way up the hill we were called to a halt to have Thanksgiving Dinner: turkey, mashed potatoes and gravy, cranberry sauce, green beans, Pumpkin pie, with lots of hot coffee. Good fare; only mushroom soup and crisp canned onion rings were missing from the green beans. This was the first of many meals to be eaten standing up, or sitting on the side of the hill. We were spaced fifteen feet apart so that a single enemy mortar round would not result in multiple casualties. We were at last in a combat zone, really earning (deserving) our extra $45.00 per month of combat pay.

One hot meal each day was delivered up the mountain by Korean men and women. Thermal containers were filled in the mess hall kitchen, at the bottom of the hill, near Company Headquarters. These containers, about twice the size of a breadbox, were carried up the mountain strapped to the backs of these food couriers, Korean civilians. They did not wear any shoes, but rather wrapped their feet in material similar to what was used to make their jackets and pants. Traction on the slippery slopes was obviously quite good using this quilted material as foot coverings. The rumor was that all of this fabric was made in China (our mutual enemy), as were their entire outfits.

Breakfast was available early at a bunker just off the trench line. Cold cereal, milk from powder, sugar, rolls, jelly, coffee. Supper was forever "C" rations, a selection of pre-cooked, canned meals, to be heated, or if conditions required, eaten at the existing temperature, indoors or outdoors. Decent tasting, quite filling. GI's were forever trading, as cans were passed out at random. The two favorites in our area were "Ham and Eggs" and "Baked Beans and Hotdog Chunks." We had plenty of canned heat (Sterno) to light and use for heating these containers. We were never issued "K" rations, which were used for forces in the field under stringent combat conditions. The rumor was that "K's" were all but inedible. I never tasted one.

Friend Jim Lagoe's last words, before we parted at the bottom of the hill on my day of arrival, had been, "it isn't too bad up there. I spent four months without serious incident." This was encouraging.

Dinner over, we proceeded to climb almost to the peak of the hill, where we encountered the G-Company trench line, dug in at the rear of a multitude of hoochies. I was sharing one with another new arrival (bunker mates names forgotten, as they changed frequently for a plethora of reasons). Bunkers were constructed of eight-foot long logs, each approximately eight inches in diameter. One layer, standing vertically, made up the walls. Two layers, laid crosswise with many sandbags atop, made up the roof, said to be able to withstand a direct hit from an enemy mortar or a misfire from one of our own supporting mortar units to our rear. On the downhill front side of the bunker were slits to fire out of, should a frontal attack ever come.

Hoochies were heated by charcoal placed in a gallon can which originally held salad oil, syrup, etc. With holes properly punched on the lower sides of the can and vented out the roof, via a round thin metal tube, the small space within the hoochie was toasty. Journalist Tom Brady wrote a book titled *The Coldest War* after spending a winter as an infantry officer in Korea. He sure got that cold part right!

A couple of weeks later, I was called off the hill for the job interview with Captain Wendt. He asked me two questions: 1. "Did he need to see me type?" I told him my typing story. That sufficed. 2. "Did I like to work with details?"

I answered *"Yes,"* and added that "I had worked as a part-time team leader in a college bookstore for two years, where dealing with details was of the essence; and I loved it!" He hired me, and told me to show up for orientation with Sgt. Lagoe at 0600 hours on January 8th. I saluted, turned on my heel, and left. A few weeks later, I obeyed the Captain, and reported to the Sergeant.

Life on the MLR (Main Line of Resistance) was routinely busy, day and night. Bunkers were constantly being improved and reinforced. Trenches were always in need of being made a bit deeper. One inch less of your head showing, above the trench line, would deter enemy snipers. Two friends, both from Kentucky, disobeyed the order not to sit on the top of the trench and were shot dead by enemy snipers, who were always present. They were our only fatal casualties while on the Ice Cream Cone. Open-air latrines needed some attention every day, as did those expended cannon shells used as urinals, embedded into the backside of the mountain (referred to as Piss Tubes).

Eating took quite a bit of time as we spread out along paths leading down the backside of the mountain. To scrub one's mess kit after each meal was a necessary task. This was done first by scraping uneaten food into a garbage can, then the entire kit, with metal silverware and cup from your water canteen hanging on, was dunked into and swirled around in scalding hot water in a large garbage can containing a heavy concentration of GI (strong) soap. Then, the whole array went into clear hot water to get rid of any soap residue. If said rinse was not performed to perfection, then after the next meal you might need to be near the latrine for a day or two. (This affliction was named the GI's.)

Showers were not available. All washing up, so to speak, was done in your steel helmet. We did lots of that, always with cold water. A large tank trailer of all-purpose water was parked just over the top of the hill, obviously on the side away from the enemy. This water was used for all things, including coffee, made each morning by two assistant cooks who lived in a bunker on the hill. They were as ready to fight as we all were. Everyone was trained to just do it, should an attack occur. Taking a complete bath out of a steel helmet in a nice warm charcoal-heated bunker is an experience everyone should have, at least once.

All of us did trench-guard duty three nights per week, the usual two hours on, two hours off regimen. We were watching, and listening, for infiltrators coming up the hill or along the trench line. That guard duty was when I first heard the password "Bubblegum." Our executive officer introduced it, saying that Asians could not master this word, and when they said it, it would be very garbled. His take was, "If you say 'Who goes there?' and you get no reply or a garbled reply of 'Bubbbleegumee,' shoot to kill." Daytime trench guards were, as always, reduced by one-half.

I remembered friend Jim Lagoe's words "it isn't too bad up there" when the order came up or down the line from Battalion, depending on how you looked at it: "contact patrols were to be immediately initiated, on a twice-weekly basis." We had all been alerted to this activity, way back in basic training. In order to ascertain precisely where the enemy was located, a patrol of one squad (eight to ten men) in this situation, should be sent down the mountain into the valley ("no man's land") until contact was made in one of three ways: 1. Draw enemy fire; 2. See the enemy, and establish coordinates; 3. Hear the enemy, and establish coordinates. I was given the *privilege* of participating in two contact patrols.

Eight of us were briefed as follows by Company Commander Capt. Wendt. In those days, only a commissioned officer could send us into harm's way. "You will be prepared to leave the east end of the trench line at 2100 hours. Proceed single file to the floor of the valley. Space yourselves circa fifteen feet apart during the descent. Do not leave the established path, except if you come under fire. This is to avoid any possibility of encountering a land mine. The hill in front of our position is mined with 'Bouncing Betties' as a defensive tactic. Stepping on one of these triggers the release of a small metal projectile to about chest high, where it explodes, sending shrapnel in all directions. This defensive instrument of land warfare maims more often than it kills." We carefully heeded Capitan Wendt's words, both going and coming back.

Because I was the BAR man, with the high-powered automatic weapon, I got to go first. There was one problem; my weapon would not fire.

Browning Automatic Rifles have a slide, which helps put the weapon into operation. The slide on my piece was burred, making it impossible to fire.

Our supply sergeant had ordered a new slide from Regiment, but it had not arrived prior to our first contact patrol. I was, however, ordered to take my BAR on patrol, operational or not. Don't ask me why. Good soldiers obey, which I did. However, I did have a sidearm—a Colt 45 semi-automatic pistol. It is referred to as a "Close Quarters Battle Weapon." Fortunately, I did not ever need to fire it. It was, however, a fearsome piece of hardware.

We proceeded down the hill into the valley. On flat ground we spread out, now walking as if on eggshells, to not alert the enemy, and to not step on a Bouncing Betty. We never did know for certain whether we were facing North Koreans or Chinese. Rumor was, if you were ever captured, hope it was a Chinese unit; they adhered to the Geneva Convention in treatment of prisoners. It was said that the North Koreans did not comply, and were cruel. It did not take too long before we heard the enemy shouting back and forth, between themselves. Our squad leader, a Sergeant with a compass, took some readings and led us back up the hill, into the trench. Hearing the enemy was interesting, even though he sounded happy. We knew nothing of their language.

G-Company, as part of the international police force, was positioned between a South Korean unit on our left flank and a Puerto Rican unit on our right flank. Neither of these forces did contact patrols. Hence, we did not need to be concerned that either of our allies were out wandering around in the valley, talking to each other in their native tongue.

It was winter, with the ground covered with snow. For our patrol we were all garbed in white cover-up pants, roomy over-blouses, and a large white skull cap over our steel helmets. Just before we left the trench and sallied down the hill, one of the guys said of our all white cover-ups, "If we had peaked caps, we might be mistaken for members of the Ku Klux Klan." Funny. No one laughed, until we were through with our mission in front of the MLR. Back in the culinary bunker, being served lots of hot coffee and warm orange-peel muffins, we could now laugh about that peaked cap joke, and we did.

My second contact patrol was only a tiny bit different. My BAR weapon was fully operational and ready to kill. The bipod on the front was locked in, but at a moment's notice it could be set up to steady this powerful automatic weapon, should I decide to be in a prone position for firing. With this weapon now ready to go, I did not mind so much being up front. Plus, I still had the Colt 45 sidearm at the ready. All BAR operators were issued this sidearm, as a BAR is difficult to turn quickly enough to defend a close in attack from either side or the rear.

The plan for this second contact patrol was to make our task in no-man's-land easier, by having our rear mortar detachment send two high-flying flares to be timed with our arrival on the valley floor. Said flares arrived a few minutes late. Hence, we were about 100 yards closer to the enemy than was planned, actually a few steps into North Korea. However, we drew no fire. We got a good look at their positions. Thus, our squad leader got an accurate plotting of the enemy's precise whereabouts. When we were back from our contact mission, having the now-traditional coffee and orange-peel muffins, mortar rounds came flying overhead toward the enemy location. Thus ended my contact with the enemy. Two days later, January 8, 1953, I left the hill for one week of orientation. On January 15th, Jim Lagoe rotated. I was now the G-Company Clerk.

Before leaving the hill, I was able to visit most everyone in my Company. Everyone wished me well, and almost all asked me to: 1. Be sure to add two combat points to their record each month. 2. To be certain Billy, the Company mailman, delivered mail every M-W-F. 3. To be certain I sent the Form for them to fill out to apply for R & R (rest and recuperation) in Japan, when they became eligible. I agreed to give those very important tasks serious attention, every day. I was now responsible for at least 144 GI's in these and other administrative areas.

At the suggestion of my mentor, former Company Clerk Jim Lagoe, I did not go on R & R. His reasoning: stay put to protect your job, your typewriter, and your health. Stories about GI's returning from six days of R & R with a variety of serious, unusual, sometimes rare, and untreatable diseases, ran rampant. As Company Clerk, he knew of what he spoke. As I gained access to all records, including medical and court marshal documents, I, too, found out that it was best to stay in Korea, even in a combat zone, and thus away from infectious diseases in Japan. Nuff said!

I now had a new job, only 1000 feet from my last job, and in the same general locale: "G" George Company Clerk, reporting to Captain Wendt.

☙

COMPANY CLERK: 1953

Being G-Company clerk had immediate and innumerable advantages.

I was housed in the Company Headquarters bunker at the bottom of the hill, along with our new Company Commander, 1st Lt. Jack Place, Executive Officer 2nd Lt. James Brandon, and Company Mailman Cpl. Billy (unremembered). Capt. Wendt had rotated.

This location was still within range of enemy mortar fire. However, it was located on the side of the hill at a very difficult angle to be reached by shells.

The bunker was the size of an extended two-car garage, built of logs like those used for hoochies on the hill. In each of the four corners of this log structure was a bunk, built by stringing "commo-wire" back and forth between a twin-bed-sized frame of 2x4's. By stringing more wire, the "mattress" could be made more firm. Placing your sleeping bag on these spring-like wires was a far cry from the dirt floor of an online bunker, with only your poncho to guard against bumpy spots, and moisture seeping into your bag and through to your body.

This reference to "commo-wire" needs a bit of explanation. Field telephones used to communicate in the field (up, down, and around the mountain, and into the valley) were packaged in a large purse-like canvas bag with a strap that placed the purse just below your hip. This bag contained a black, French style Bell Telephone receiver and two heavy duty batteries. This was not a cell phone or a radio-phone.

Connecting to other phones in the field required wire. New wire was usually laid for each mission, then abandoned. Hence, we could harvest it, very carefully, to avoid land mines. Wire had a multitude of uses, not the least of which was the manufacture of mattresses.

I had forgotten that my first assignment, after I arrived at the Ice Cream Cone, was a day at Regimental Headquarters learning to lay communications wire. It was always to be placed redundantly, two wires stretched circa four to six feet apart. Thus, a mortar shell which exploded nearby was less likely to take out both strands. After that day of commo-wire training, I was never called upon to use it. Then again, neither was I ever called on to use my CBR training, received at Sasebo, Japan. Thank heavens on both counts.

The job of Company Clerk was interesting, demanding, satisfying, and often fun. Up at 0500 hours every day. Coffee had already been brought from the mess hall by "Charlie," the Company Commander's houseboy. Charlie was assigned to our Company by the KATUSHA (Korean Augmentation To The United States Army). This was a branch of the ROK (Republic Of [South] Korea Army). Charlie was smart. Before the war began, he had been an English teacher in a private girls' school in Seoul. His English was a great example for all of us.

Charlie kept the bunker spotless. He kept the two officers in clean, pressed clothes, with boots shined. He brought all our meals from the kitchen bunker next door. The mess sergeant was very good to us; that meant he was really good to the officers. Joyfully, Billy, the mailman, and I tagged along.

I cut a deal with Charlie regarding my clothes and boots. He earned a big bundle of U.S. (script) dollars on the side. Thus, I had more time to do my clerk work. That paid off with a fast promotion from Cpl. to Sgt. (three stripes up – one down). I would like to call this a battlefield promotion. But "Keep truth on your side" my maternal Grandmother often said. It wasn't such a promotion.

A gunmetal gray typewriter-stand and a letter-sized four-drawer black metal file faced the wall at the head of my bed. I had a footlocker at the bottom of my bed, and room to hang a few garments from a metal pipe above my bed. Comforts galore, and a perfect spot for my *million-dollar* typewriter, worth its weight in gold, many times over. Just like my buddy Jim said it would be. Plus, I had the biggest and brightest lamp in the command post. It hung off the log wall over the typewriter stand. Oh yes, we had lights from a small—but quite powerful—generator located in a large metal casing next to the mess hall.

First duty, after breakfast circa 0600 hours, was to read communiqués from both Battalion and Regiment that had been delivered during the evening and night, plus any information from our Company forces on the hill. An important part of my job was to decide what information to pass on to the company commander or executive officer. That accomplished, I prepared the all-important Morning Report. This document had to account for all personnel assigned to our Company, about

130 troops, eight cadre. Where was everyone? TD—Temporary Duty; SC—Sick Call @ Battalion; H—Hospital @ Regiment; I&R—Japan; ROT—Rotating; MIA—Missing in Action; WIA—Wounded in Action; KIA—Killed in Action; AWOL—Away without Leave. These numbers were to be in the hands of the Battalion Commander by 0700 hours. Delivery was by field telephone to the Battalion Sergeant Major. Believe it—they were always on time.

First Lt. Place and Second Lt. Brandon frequently spent time on the hill with the non-commissioned officers, inspecting weapons, sighting the enemy to the front, scanning the valley with high-powered binoculars, planning for troop replacements to be integrated into a particular squad or platoon, inspecting bunker fortifications, and many other details intended to maximize the effectiveness of our response, should a frontal attack occur. Upon their return from these inspections, I interpreted their notes, typed them up, and obtained approval before sending them to Battalion via a courier.

Administrative details were endless. Orders for supplies, including all foodstuffs for the mess hall crew, ammunition, weapon replacements and parts, clothing and boots. The latter went from leather to "Mickey Mouse" boots, so called (unofficially) because they resembled Disney's cartoon character's shoes. This was a new development: two layers of rubber, with a layer of wool in between. Frozen feet would be all but a thing of the past, if the wearer kept a pair of socks inside his shirt lying against his chest, and changed to these now dry socks at least once per day. "Mickey's" footwear, for combat infantrymen in cold climates, was a miracle. The Parke-Davis Corporation, a Detroit, Michigan, pharmaceutical business, was deeply involved in the development of this foot-saving footwear. One other responsibility was to order whisky and beer rations for the officers. First Lt. Place convinced me to try a shot of whiskey (Old Grandad). I did, and said, "Well, I will never have to do that again." Mailman Billy and I were awarded a few beers, always at room temperature.

I had just one "employee," Billy the Mailman. His job was very important to everyone in the company. He made five trips per week to Battalion to pick up our mail. He sorted it by person, and lined it up in cardboard boxes, in the sequence of bunker locations. Occasionally, I would be recruited to join Billy to help with in-trench, hootchie-by-hootchie delivery. This was usually on a Monday, when incoming mail was the heaviest, having had the weekend to accumulate at Battalion. A trip up the hill was exciting. A jeep driver arrived to pick us up, circa 2200 hours. It was pitch dark, unless the moon decided to pop out. Up the mountain road, with no side barriers on the ridge line. If there was a moon, danger from enemy snipers. If no moon, danger from going off the road by just one foot, and ending up in the valley below—certain death. However, these jeep drivers were all formidable, and then some.

Everything in George Company was running smoothly. I received a bit of honest, sincere appreciation from my boss, First Lt. Place. Of course, I humbly accepted same. However, the saying in all branches of military service is "expect a SNAFU" (situation normal all fouled up). "Fouled" is sometimes changed to a different word, depending on the audience. Orders arrived from Division HQ. (General Clark Ruffner) via Regiment and then Battalion. G-Company was to move to a new holding position, this time on Heartbreak Ridge. This was a much longer frontage to hold, but included two additional companies. It was only about one mile to the east of our current position, at a slightly higher elevation. The valley out front was wider. Our current position would be manned by a new unit from the Republic Of Korea Army.

Planning for this move began immediately, although the move date was still one month away. Logistics would be challenging for everyone. Planning meetings, with the officers, non-coms, mess sergeant, supply sergeant, and me, were frequent and long. Along the trench line, every other bunker would be vacated. That force would then move via personnel carriers to Heartbreak, and move into "every other" bunker just vacated. Where that contingent was moving to was never divulged. The second wave from the Ice Cream Cone would then be trucked to Heartbreak and complete the new front. Meanwhile, the ROK (South Korean) troops would be moving into these positions, just vacated by G-Company. Sounds easy? It wasn't, especially communicating with the new Ice Cream Cone tenants. Charlie the houseboy helped a bit, when translation was needed. Executive Officer Second Lt. Brandon was a fantastic planner. He had graduated from the Oklahoma State University ROTC program with a commission and a degree in mechanical engineering. He engineered this in-combat move to perfection.

Moving to Heartbreak Ridge felt weird, having heard about the intense fighting which occurred at that venue in September and October 1951. It seemed like this was hallowed ground. We did not have to win it; just hold it. We did.

Our new company headquarters was pretty much the same, though a bit larger. I had a little alcove for my one piece of office furniture. I had always sat on a large wooden box. No change here. Billy had a built-in sorting rack, with a lot of cubbyholes. The officers had a small plotting table. The one top-flight addition was the availability of a shower, of sorts. Charlie, who moved along with us to the new position, worked it out with two of his civilian friends. Just across the road was a tiny box-like structure of tent canvass, 2x4s, and cardboard, with a flap entrance. Inside, a #10 tin can hung from the ceiling on several cords. Into this can ran water from a little stream, which Charlie's buddies had directed into a wooden trough that looked like a very long miter box. The water ran into and out of the can, which had many holes punched in the bottom. The water temperature depended on the day, sunny or cloudy. You stepped under the flow and got wet—stepped out—soaped-up—stepped back under and rinsed. You had already paid your fifty cents. This contraption was available all day and beyond, upon request. Very primitive, but a great alternative to the steel helmet routine. As the weather warmed, the "can-shower" became the center of the universe for all of us not on the hill.

All troops were settled into their new locations. It was mid-May 1953. Things were going well. Inspections seemed a bit more stringent, reports longer, contact patrols more frequent, rumors more in-depth, guard duty more alerted, supply problems more challenging. Hot meals were still taken up this higher hill by Korean civilians. Food was still very tasty. Rumor of a cease fire/armistice became stronger, and continued day in and day out.

An order came from Battalion that we were to participate in a front-wide "Turkey Shoot." Company G had, in fact participated in two of these activities while on the Ice Cream Cone. Nothing changed. At the given hour, shortly after the evening meal of C-rations, every member of the Company gathered on the hill with their particular weapon, ready to fire over the top of the trench out into "no man's land." A certain number of rounds were allocated for each type of firearm. M-1 rifle—one clip, BAR—one half clip,

Carbine—one half banana clip, sidearm 45 automatic—four rounds. Mortar units participated by preparing to fire (loading blanks), following all routines short of firing live ammo— air cooled machine guns—two bursts. The Company commander fired a single shot, at a prescribed time. Then, as planned, all hell broke loose for circa one minute. The purpose was threefold: 1. Test each weapon. 2. Create a reason to clean every weapon, bringing it up to inspectable condition. 3. Be certain all troops were ready, willing, and able to fire. In battle, it is well known that getting even well-trained soldiers to fire their weapons is sometimes iffy. Turkey Shoots hopefully helped, in part at least, to remedy that deficiency before it occurred. Very noisy, for a bit. The next few days we used up lots of cleaning fluid, lubricating oil, and little flannel patches to run up and down weapon bores.

Then the long-rumored event came true. At precisely 10:00 A.M., on July 27, 1953, a "cease fire" was signed at the Panmungom conference center, at or near the Thirty-eighth Parallel. Both parties agreed to leave their positions across the entire peninsula. That meant that many thousands of U.S. troops and all allies, most notably South Koreans, were moving out as well. The logistics were mind-boggling.

However, even before the move had begun, somehow an order was given to use up live mortar ammunition by firing into enemy lines, all across the front. The rumor was that the "lazy Americans" started it, to avoid having to transport those tons of ammunition off the hill. The Americans, of course claimed the same thing about the Chinese/North Korean combine. In my opinion, no one will never know for certain. Everyone took to their bunkers.

However, G-Company Commander Place and his Executive Officer Brandon did not make it. They had been up on the hill with high-powered binoculars, surveying the enemy lines. A mortar shell hit nearby, injuring them both. The Medics were on the spot quickly, and both leaders were taken to the Regimental hospital. Sadly, First Lt. Place lost his left arm below the elbow; Second Lt. Brandon lost his life. The morning report, dated July 28, 1953, carried a KIA and a WIA. "Poignant," does not come anywhere close when remembering this distressing event. That was my last ever Morning Report.

The senior Master Sergeant came down from the hill (three stripes, both up and down). He took command of G-Company. He called together our mess sergeant, supply sergeant, mailman cpl., and company clerk sergeant (me). We got the troops moved back to Battalion, and a few to Regiment.

We stayed two more nights, then joined the troops. Battalion logistics were being run by Mr. Horner, a Warrant Officer (non-commissioned). He was a master organizer. Orders were being posted from his office hourly, sending troops in all directions. I gave him my Royal typewriter, the stand, and even the one remaining unused typewriter ribbon. We were all housed in tents. We walked around looking for buddies, read paperbacks, ate, and talked, mostly about what we thought had been a "war," not a police action. Then we began to thin out, via the train, which would take us south to a ship bound for the U.S.A. My orders were posted. Amazingly, I had been promoted to Sergeant First Class (three stripes up and two down). Lt. Place probably never knew that the approval had arrived from Division. I had typed the application at his direction, a month or so before. We picked up our duffle bags from the Battalion supply sergeant. He had kept them as promised, with our non-combat gear inside.

I boarded the train with orders for the Busan supply depot. Had been there on the way up. I arrived. Spent one night. No guard duty. Boarded the USS Begor, a dual-purpose ship, both a high-speed transport and destroyer escort. Built by the Defoe Ship-building Company, Bay City, Michigan. The ship was heading for dry-dock for upkeep somewhere in the States. We would be deposited at San Francisco, whence we had departed ten months before. That had been on a huge troopship. The Begor was not a troopship, and was able to accommodate only fifty of us.

I had been a Fireman going over. I had no duty assigned on the way back. Do not know how much faster we went back, compared to going over; but it was for certain a faster, bumpier sail. We had no rousing band to meet us, like we had when leaving. We could have cared less. The USS Begor glided quietly into a very large slip. We were back in the States.

I stayed at Camp Stoneman for a few days. No visit from Cousins Jack and Merry, who were in Russia on business, representing the Society of Automotive Engineers. Jack was Association President that year. My orders were cut for Fort Sheridan, Illinois, near Chicago, from where I would be discharged. The cross-country trip was very interesting. It was slow, as the troop train did not have right-of-way clearance. Hence, we spent time on sidings while awaiting the passing of the more highly-rated commercial freight and passenger trains. Nothing bothered us; we were going home.

I arrived at Fort Sheridan August 23, 1953. I had a top-to-bottom physical. The next day included a brief debriefing by an Army Intelligence Officer.

I had been offered a promotion to Master Sergeant (three stripes up and three down) while still in Korea. This required a three-year re-enlistment. I had declined that opportunity. I got the chance to decline again, and did. On September 1, 1953, I was presented with an honorable discharge, a train ticket to the Detroit, Michigan, Central Depot, and a handshake from a high-ranking officer.

I arrived in Detroit. Took a Checker Taxi to 87 Grove Avenue, Highland Park, Michigan. I had left there twenty-three months and eleven days earlier.

The taxi stopped, double parked, fortunately blocking oncoming traffic, because wife-to-be Ginny was sitting on a neighbor's porch across the street from my house. She saw the flashing lights on the taxi, and looking neither right or left, dashed across the street into my arms. Now, I was really home. And I needed to begin looking for work.

☙

GROUP INSURANCE SALESMAN: 1953

My honorable discharge, on September 1, 1953, was forty-nine days before the two years of military service I had been drafted to serve were complete. Later, I discovered that this tiny fact meant that it would be easier for the Army to recall me to active duty. My MOS (Military Occupational Specialty) was 1745. This military identifier was always in high demand. It translated to "squad leader," even though my final six months of service in Korea had been as a company clerk, in a combat unit. My rank was Sergeant First Class.

I thought about this, using the "worst possible case scenario." Should there be another police action, or a war, and I were called back to duty, would I be able to lead a squad into combat? My combat resume said yes. I agreed.

However, all of that was now behind me. I was ready to begin life as a civilian. Wife-to-be Ginny and I set a date for our wedding—January 23, 1954. We would both be twenty-five years old. Eight days later, I would be twenty-six. However, what I was eager to do was get a job and begin a career. My undergraduate degree from Michigan State College was a BS in B&PS (Business & Public Service—later renamed Business Administration). This included a minor in Insurance. Four courses made it an insurance minor: Life, Property/Casualty, Statistics, and Business Law. To be certain I understood it, I had repeated Statistics, and still only achieved a "B" grade.

So, with the insurance business as my goal, I called Russell H. Moore, who had been my Life Insurance instructor at MSC in 1950-51. He had at that time suggested I contact him after I was discharged. He was gracious. His first words were, "thank you for serving." I had never heard those words before. Nice. He asked where Ginny and I planned to live. He agreed to call me back within one week, after he had surveyed the insurance job market in the Detroit area. He called four days later, recommending that I call R.T. Johnstone, Michigan President of Marsh & McLennan, one of the largest insurance agents in the country. Mr. Moore was a friend of R.T. M&M was expanding their Group Insurance department, hence there was an opening for a sales representative.

I called Mr. Johnstone. Very pleasant chap. He would set up an interview for me with Jack Porter, manager of the Group Insurance Department. This was on the strength of my recommendation from his good friend Russ Moore. Jack Porter called the next day. We set up a face-to-face meeting for Tuesday of the following week. We met in the M&M conference room of their thirteenth floor office, First National Bank Building, on Woodward Avenue in downtown Detroit.

We had a lengthy visit, mostly concerning what I had done in the Army. Also, what courses I had pursued in college at Michigan State. Mr. Porter explained what the job involved as a salaried group insurance agent. He also explained that the majority of M&M group insurance customers were outstate, especially in western Michigan. The reason for this was that group policies were built around hospital-medical insurance. In the Detroit area Blue Cross–Blue Shield had the market sewn up, with auto industry policies bargained for with the UAW.

Our discussion ended with Jack saying that he was ready to offer me the position, starting at $250.00 per month, with a $25.00 increase when I married and an additional $25.00 per month when I had been with the firm six months. However, before he could put this in writing, he would have to set up an interview for me with their corporate psychologist. This person lived and worked out of their Cleveland, Ohio, office. He would not be in the Detroit area for the next two weeks. I probably showed disappointment, because all of a sudden Jack stood up, slammed the table with the flat of his hand, and said; "Damn it—you are hired. I am not going to wait for that shrink again. Are you able to start the first Monday in October?" I said "yes." He had gone over the benefits. They appeared excellent to me. He gave me a booklet explaining each one. We shook hands. He saw me to the big glass door, through which I had entered a couple of hours before. My career had begun.

The M&M Group Department was not large. Each member (all males) had a nickname. I didn't know who bestowed these monikers. Manager—Jack Porter (Jovial Jack), Research Supervisor—Clyde Goodrich (Cognizant Clyde), Marketing Manager—Harry Leathers (High-dollar Harry), Life and Annuity Manager—Mel (not remembered), Life Insurance Salesman—Dave Kelly (Downtown Dave), Russ Vahlbusch—Group Insurance Salesman—(Rusty Russ). The working atmosphere was friendly. No one seemed tense, or pressured. This was a very large office, taking up an entire floor of a huge office building. M&M represented a multitude of insurance companies, offering every type of insurance available. The Group staff was one of the smallest.

The work was interesting. I reported to Clyde Goodrich, with a dotted line to Harry Leathers. My initial task was to research and then develop group insurance rates for a foundry in Albion, Michigan. From this work would come a proposal to be presented to the Foundry Board of Directors. I was working with masses of data: number of employees, ages, sex, ethnicity, race, job descriptions. I was coordinating with several insurance companies, each wishing to compete for a piece of this business. The research ended. My boss Clyde, with me learning alongside him, put together a benefits analysis to present to these several insurance companies to obtain their premium offers for proposed coverages of employees at the foundry. This was one-half of my new job. The other part was to present (sell) the proposal to the client. Harry Leathers was to take me in tow and teach me to do this part of the job. We visited the foundry in Albion, and I watched and listened (marveled, really) at how

Harry presented this package to the Board. They signed on the dotted line.

Harry had picked me up at our apartment, 418 Savanah West, Detroit, Michigan, a few blocks north of Six-Mile Road, at 7:00 A.M. for the drive to Albion for our 10:30 A.M. appointment. We had a quick burger in Albion. When the meeting was over, he took me directly home, arriving circa 3:30 P.M. Nice.

October and November had been busy. December tailed off. The group department expected this, because "businesses seldom arrange new insurance contracts just before Christmas." During that month we updated files, and there were many that had not been looked at for some time.

I was settling in. Clyde introduced me to his friend Jake Blow, from the property and casualty department. The three of us ate our brown bag lunches together in the conference room, where I had been interviewed and Jack had slapped the table. Occasionally, on Fridays, we planned to not "brown bag" it, but rather walk to the famous Broadway Market for lunch. I was taught how to construct a sandwich. 1. Purchase an onion roll at the bakery stall. 2. Holding the roll on a piece of waxed paper, purchase my choice of lunch meat (and or cheese) at the Deli counter to add to the roll (occasionally a Kosher dill pickle). 3. Walk over to the dairy counter to choose a carton of milk, chocolate milk, or orangeade. You then needed to sneak down to the end of the dairy counter. The nice lady there would bring a large pot of yellow mustard out from under the counter, and slop it on your sandwich, until you said, "enough." Illegal, since she did not have a restaurant license. But tasty.

Our department leader, Jack, threw a Christmas party at his home in Royal Oak, on Bamlet street, between Twelve and Thirteen Mile Roads, one block off Woodward, in Royal Oak. Nice party, including all of his staff and some folks from his neighborhood.

Jake Blow invited me to join the insurance league bowling team. I did. We bowled at the State Fair alleys on Woodward avenue, between Seven and Eight Mile Roads. Wives were always on hand to keep score and urge us to victory. Clyde and wife Helma invited us to their home, along with Jake and wife Gen, to play Monopoly, eat popcorn, and drink Coca Cola. They lived on the east side of Detroit, just south of Eight-Mile Road. We went. Then Jake and Gen had the same outing. They lived in Mt. Clemens. Then we reciprocated.

Dave Kelly invited us to his home in Birmingham for dinner. His wife (name unremembered) made excellent lobster bisque. I loved it. Ginny choked it down. We were becoming entrenched in the business and some social happenings.

The month of January, 1954, was busy at the office, getting a proposal ready to present to Gerber Products Company in Fremont, Michigan. At that time their main product was baby food. They were extending the production line, adding employees, and beginning to use technology in order to let the Marketing Vice President know every morning how many cases of "pureed green peas" were in every warehouse, nationwide.

The meeting included Gerber Products president Dan Gerber, vice president Steve Nisbet, Gerber insurance department manager (name forgotten), plus Robert D. Bristol, manager of the new communications systems department.

Bob Bristol was my brother-in-law. He had lived in Fremont, Michigan, working for the Gerber corporation for several years. His current assignment was to create that daily call-in system to inform officers and sales managers about the peas. Insurance requirements were changing fast, right along with these innovations. Marsh & McLennan was ready to cover all new "exposures," as coverages were referred to in the insurance industry.

These additions required changes in all areas of insurance. Marsh & Mac was their insurance agent of choice. Incidentally, it was rumored that president R.T. Johnstone was in his high-level position because he had delivered the Ford Motor Co. account to Marsh & Mac, for several lines of insurance. Ford self-insured for fire. However, there were numerous other lines, including business interruption insurance. Whether the rumor was true or not, R.T. was the only one allowed to contact Ford. BTW, what those R.T. initials stood for I never discovered.

I asked for the Friday before our January 23rd wedding, and the Monday and Tuesday after, as days off. Granted. I returned as planned and began to put the finishing touches on the Gerber proposal. From that moment on my career in the insurance business began slowly to fall apart. I asked my boss, Clyde, to remind his boss, Jack, to remind treasurer, Bea Mac Vicar, that, with my January wedding completed, I was now to begin earning $275.00 per month. The word came back that Jack would like to talk with me. He did. It had been decided that this was not possible, as it had never been done before. Jack admitted that in his desire to hire me he had made that promise, which he was now unable to keep. However, I would receive, that increase along with the promised $25.00 at the end of my six months. I asked the clerk typist, Delores Del Dona, who sat directly in front of my desk, how long she had worked for M&M, and what her base salary was. It was $300.00 per month. She had been an employee for one year.

A young fellow named Cliff Phalen joined the department next to us. His boss was Dick (last name not remembered). He had one other subordinate, John Feddick. They were both actuaries serving all departments. Cliff was a junior business administration student at Princeton University. He was on a six-month internship with Marsh & Mac. His parents lived in Bloomfield Hills. He was to move from department to department. I invited him to join me on a Friday for a sampling of fare at the Broadway Market, booth by booth. We went together the first time, then he joined the group and loved the experience. We talked about a lot of things, and especially the east. He had grown up in the New Jersey/New York area.

One lunch hour he asked me if I was making insurance my career. I said yes, that my academic prep was aimed at doing that. However, I said that I had just begun working for M&M in October. He said, you should take a look at the Telephone Company. They have many good management jobs available, because they are so big: thirty thousand employees in Michigan, and three quarters of a million nationwide. He continued, "my dad has worked for Ma Bell for many years." My response was, "What does he do?" "He is the President of Michigan Bell, transferred from AT&T in New York. If you ever think that you would be interested, let me know, and I will ask him who you should call." I said, "Thank you for that." That ended the conversation.

The Gerber presentation went well. I got to do some of the complex explanations in front of the group. Harry did the close. On the trip home from Fremont, circa 160 miles, Harry wanted to stop for dinner at Schuler's in Marshall, Michigan. I did not want to stop, with my bride awaiting my arrival. However, I did report to him, albeit on a dotted line. Plus, I was after all just beginning my career. We stopped. I had a Stroh's beer. Harry had a couple of stronger beverages. Dinner over, we moved on toward home. Harry wanted to stop at one of his favorite watering holes (Peter Angels was the name, at Telegraph and Eight-Mile Road). I did not want to stop. We did. I had a plain 7-Up. We got to our apartment, circa three hours later than a direct trip would have taken. Harry insisted on coming in for a nightcap. Ginny had met him at Jack's Christmas party. He was probably a little fuzzy. I gave him a Carling's Black Label, brewed in Frankenmuth, Michigan. He left. (Note: five years later, High Dollar Harry was in a devastating automobile accident. He received closed head injuries, and remained a "vegetable" for the rest of his life.)

Even with these two negative experiences, I did enjoy the work. I believed that I could learn to be an effective salesman, though one a bit more subdued and cerebral than Harry, my assigned mentor.

April 1st arrived. I opened my pay envelope to view my new $300.00 rate.

Alas, it was only $275.00. I worked my way through Clyde, to Jack, who sent me to the accountant/treasurer Bea McVicar (called by all, behind her back, McFrugal). The reason she gave for my not being awarded my $50.00 per month increase was, "That would be a 20% increase, and we just do not do that here." I explained Jack's promise, before I was hired, and the second promise when the first one was not kept. Who could I complain to? Bea called in VP Peter Gossip—second in command, after R.T. Very tall, former basketball player at some small eastern college. He reiterated Mc Frugal's position. I said thank you, and shook his hand. Turned on my heel and left.

Back at my desk, being as loud as possible, I called the information operator, and asked for the telephone number for the Michigan State College placement office. I called and asked for Jack Shingleton. Jack was the epitome of a placement director. He was known nationwide for innovative processes to get graduates and alumni hired into top-flight positions. I had gotten to know Jack during the two years I worked for the MSC bookstore setting up textbook requisitions for veterans, while he was working on getting them part-time campus jobs. I got Jack on the line.

I explained that the position Russ Moore had guided me into was not working out. He was in a luncheon club with Russ. No problem; he would pull my file, and put two or three job opportunity postcards in the mail the next day. Prospective employers would not be notified. I would need to tell them the source of the referral. I gave him my home address. He wished me well in my job search, and added that if none of these first three worked out, I should call him again. I felt much better. My boss, Clyde, must have heard it all. He graciously said nothing. After all he was my Monopoly buddy.

Four days later, our mail box received three postcards, each initialed Jack S. under the MSC logo. Postcard 1—Van Wert Aviation, Van Wert, Ohio; Postcard 2—National Cash Register—Pontiac, Michigan; Postcard 3 – Michigan Bell Telephone Company—Detroit, Michigan. I began to believe in omens. Here it was: MBT president's son Cliff Whalen, Jr., had told me about management jobs at his dad's company, and out of the blue, here it was, just like the pink flint arrowhead. The next morning, I called the telephone number on the Michigan Bell card. Bruce Osgood answered. I would later learn that telephone company managers were strongly encouraged to answer their own telephones. Mr. Osgood was the district manager, responsible for recruiting and selection of management employees.

He set up an appointment for me in his office, for the following Tuesday morning at 9:00 A.M. We would have a brief interview. I would take a test, lasting about one hour. Then we would talk a bit more. He asked me to bring my birth certificate, Social Security card, and Army Report of Separation form.

I arrived fifteen minutes early. Took the quite lengthy test. I can remember only one question from that experience. How many horses were there in the United States, in 1880? This was in a group of multiple choice questions. I do not remember the choices. There was also a group of true and false questions, as well as fill-in-the-blanks. Test over. I sat in a chair opposite Mr. Osgood. On the wall in back of him was a life-size colored print of a man sitting at a large desk. He was facing a man sitting in a visitors chair, just like I was at that moment. Only his back was visible. The caption, in large bold italics read: ***In ten years, which side of the desk do you want to be sitting on?*** It was for certain another omen. I was hooked. If I was fortunate enough to receive a job offer, I was going to accept.

Bruce suggested that I call him Bruce. I would hear from him within one week. I didn't. Three days into the next week, I called him. The woman

I talked to had been the person who administered my test. When the test time was up she had ushered me into Bruce's office. She was really with it. She said, let me check the files on the desk. We have a new district manager, Mr. Bergman. He took over the district when Mr. Osgood left. I brazenly asked, "Where did he go?" She said, "I guess it is no secret; he moved to Boyne City to work for his brother-in-law in his automobile dealership." I thought, I hope this is not a different kind of omen. It wasn't. My new friend said, "I will put your file on top, and tell Mr. Bergman that you had fallen through the cracks during the changeover."

Mr. Bergman called the next day apologizing. I had passed the first round.

I now needed to be interviewed by three departments, which Bruce had selected for me based on my areas of interest. These were Commercial, Accounting, and Traffic. Departments made job offers. Personnel only did the facilitation. Appointments were set for one day the following week. I would do all three interviews that day, beginning at 9:00 A.M.— Traffic department, interview by Mr. McCracken; 12:00 noon, lunch—Accounting, with an interview by Mr. Russ Driver; and 2:00 P.M.—Commercial, with an interview conducted by Mr. Rennie Linden. It all happened as planned. In-depth questions about my previous work life. Long term goals. Very interesting. These gentlemen were seemingly very happy with their company, all with many years of service. (Note: Bruce Osgood only stayed in Boyne City three years. Michigan Bell took him back into the Marketing Department, although as a manager, down a level from his previous position as district manager.)

I returned to Mr. Bergman's office, as planned. He had received word from all three departments. Accounting did not tender me a job offer. I had been honest with Mr. Driver, admitting that accounting was not my favorite subject in college. As it turned out there was not much accounting going on. What was just beginning was computerization of everything in sight. I was not interested in that either. That left Traffic and Commercial. Both of those departments tendered me an offer. I selected Commercial for a very selfish reason. Traffic managers, like all employees in that department, were often called on to work all shifts: 24/7/365.

My start date was July 6, 1954. I was to report to Mr. Otto Bauer, in the Commercial Personnel Department, on the sixteenth floor of the Bell

Building, 1365 Cass Avenue, Detroit, Michigan. I would be signing necessary papers for Income Tax, FICA, and any other requested deductions. My starting salary would be paid weekly by check—gross $78.00. ($339.30 monthly—a 23% increase over my Marsh & MacLennan rate.) That morning, I would be told which of the seven Detroit Commercial Districts would be my home for the next year. My title was to be "College Trainee." I was very enthusiastic about working for "Ma Bell." As I left that gigantic building, walking through the multi-storied lobby, I had a single thought—what a great company this must be, and I am to be a part of it.

I was outside of Mr. Bauer's office twenty minutes early. He was already there.

His secretary met me, and shared that he had just returned from a two-week vacation trip to Mexico. She met with him behind the glass in his office.

She brought him up to date, because he did not know about me. His first question was, "Where is he supposed to work; maybe in Vinewood?" I knew where all the districts were from my interview with Mr. Linden. I was hoping for either Woodward or Webster, as any other location would require an immediate purchase of a second auto. More conversation, behind the glass. A call was made to Andy Klein in Vinewood; he apparently said no; the newest College Trainee was to go to Earl Morrow's Webster district. The interview with Mr. Bauer was interesting but brief. We established that he and his family were long-time members of the Royal Oak First Presbyterian Church where Ginny and I had been attending for a few months and were considering joining. Otto gave me a sales pitch (Ministry of Invitation) as all church members are encouraged to do. In time we did join. Note: When I had worked for Michigan Bell Telephone Company for less than a year, Otto left the company. He had purchased a small-town newspaper in Pigeon, Michigan. He stayed with that endeavor for circa three years. Returned to MBT, again as a district manager, this time in a line organization in Royal Oak, not in the cushy staff job in Corporate headquarters. He managed that new job very well. I attended his retirement some years later, along with the minister from our church.

I had taken the Woodward Avenue street car to downtown Detroit and walked the three blocks to the Bell Building. We talked about transportation to my new location and that I had used public transportation that day and noted that I would be able to do the same to get to Webster into the future.

When I think back to that next moment, I cannot help smiling. A district manager in this huge Company welcoming a new college trainee into a management development position, asking his secretary to "rustle up a couple of bus tickets for Russell." I took the tickets and walked over to the Grand River avenue bus stop. Got on board to travel to the very first of many offices I would inhabit during the next thirty-four years, five months, twenty-four days, working at the "Phone Factory." When that first day ended, I called wife Ginny and explained the complex route she would need to travel to pick me up at Webster, on Oakman Blvd. at Grand River Avenue. My career was for certain re-launched, far away from the insurance business.

ଔ

MICHIGAN BELL TELEPHONE COMPANY

COLLEGE TRAINEE: 1954

The Webster Commercial District was to be my Michigan Bell Telephone Company business home for the next twelve months. This office was located at Oakman Boulevard and Grand River Avenue in northwest Detroit. It was a one-story building that previously had been a large supermarket. It was July 6, 1954.

I entered the front door into what was called the "public office." This was where residential and small business customers could come to transact telephone company business if they were unable to do so on the telephone.

A nice lady named Betty Cook, wearing white gloves, arose and took me back into a huge office. She turned me over to Nancy Pearsall, secretary to district manager Earl Morrow, who was to be my mentor. Mr. Morrow would "be back soon." He was expecting me. I sat in his office looking out through glass into a large room filled with desks, each sitting next to huge tubs of records. At each position sat a woman ranging from young to middle-aged. At desks along the wall sat three men. No telephones were ringing. However, lights were flashing indicating that calls were arriving at a steady pace. It was quite an overwhelming sight. I would learn to understand it all and love it.

Mr. Morrow arrived. We had a long visit. He welcomed me. It turned out he had worked at the *Detroit News* for two summers when he was a student at the University of Michigan. He had met my dad. Mr. Morrow had worked in the circulation truck delivery section right next to the Mailing Department where my dad was the superintendent. His dad was Ernie Morrow. Ernie operated a fleet of green-colored stake trucks delivering newspapers to numerous suburban locations plus a few outstate. It turned out that my dad and his dad had been friends for many years. Ernie had a contract arrangement with the *News*. Newspapers for the most part were delivered by company-owned and operated red-and-white trucks. Each truck had a driver and a jumper. The jumper's job was to grab the number of papers to be left at a location, jump off, run them into the drugstore, beer store, or wherever they had orders. It was a physically demanding and dangerous job running between parked cars. Earl said the money had been good for a college student.

With "getting to know you" out of the way, Mr. Morrow went over an outline of what the next twelve months would be like for me. The next week I would be in the cash office with supervisor Jean Cevellen. The following week I would work in the order room with supervisor Argie Loyasis. The week thereafter I would begin an eight-week course to become a Business Office Service Representative (SR). Training would be conducted by the district training supervisor, Mrs. Alberta Peckham. The training room was outfitted with standard desks and tubs with mock-ups of customer service and billing records. These were for use in simulating incoming customer order and billing calls.

I would have a newly hired "tub mate" named Jackie Cantile, who was also in SR training. During this training period I would report to the Miscellaneous Manager, Dick Weth. When my training was complete, I would be an SR; on-line handling live incoming customer calls in Business Office Supervisor (BOS) Kay Getson's Section, in manager Bob Salton's Unit. This would continue for about two months. I would then be assigned to a Section as a BOS with six SRs and one file clerk reporting to me. At that time I would be moved to manager Don Rennick's Unit. This first leadership role (BOS) would last about four months.

However, before I took over this Section, I would receive basic supervisory training in the corporate headquarters building, 1365 Cass Avenue, in downtown Detroit. I opined that the planning was very impressive. Earl said, "Thank you for that." He continued with what was to be the first of a multitude of homey company sayings: "*We like to plan our work; and work our plan.*" He continued, "come to see me at any time you have questions or needs that you cannot get handled through your manager. I am your mentor. All our management personnel are OK with having you, a college trainee, in their midst. They are aware that one day you may well be their district manager."

It all happened pretty much as planned. Miss Cantile and I both graduated on time with satisfactory appraisals. We went to work as SRs, although in different units. I had a new tub mate, Elaine Jardine. All SRs had been trained to sell additional telephone services "whenever there was an opportunity," whatever that meant. We were supposed to look for these chances to sell extension telephones ($2.50 to install, $1.10 per month, with a one-party line; $.95 per month with a two-party line). We should also offer French-style telephones in ivory, green, and melon, at $5.00 for the instrument, plus the installation charge. Suggesting an additional listing in the white pages for family members was a must at $.35 per month.

Elaine and I made a deal. I could not keep up with my filing. She would help me stay current with filing, as she was speedy beyond belief. I, for my part, would go on break with her and give her tips and encouragement on what to say to customers to make sales. She was not skilled at selling. I was inept at filing. She kept my filing up to date. She in turn achieved enough sales to stay afloat. Mostly she had been reluctant to ask the customer to buy, after having described the product benefits. As it turned out she had grown up in Highland Park, within three blocks of where I had grown up. We had attended the same grade school, though I had been there more than ten years before she arrived.

Our tubs were outfitted with customer records that contained a listing of all services on each customer's premises. The bill related to these services was in a file right next to this light-yellow Service Application Card (SAC). Telephone calls from customers or potential customers were to be treated with great respect. SR handling of incoming customer calls was measured using a set of tough standards. These were dictated by our owner, AT&T. The defining chapter and verse: "*Tell the truth and keep promises.*" This axiom was translated into measurements of Accuracy, Completeness, and Timeliness.

If an SR gave a customer inaccurate information, e.g. an incorrect rate for a service; that was scored as an ERROR; if the customer was not given complete information, e.g. not told about the $5.00 installation charge, that was deemed an IRREGULARITY; if the SR did not retrieve the customer's record from the tub file and return to the line in a maximum of 60 seconds that was scored as a DELAY. The timeliness measurement also included a SLOW ATTENTION component. The speed by which each incoming call was answered by an SR was recorded in the Traffic Department. Having the proper number of trained SRs on position with their keys open to accept incoming calls was a complicated business problem, having to do with hiring, training, scheduling, supervising, and record keeping, and the ability to estimate call volumes by day and hour.

In addition to these stringent performance standards, five more standards were measured. These were collectively called TONE, which included: Speech, Understanding, Explanation, Attitude, and Courtesy. To some extent these were subjective judgments: _Speak_ clearly at a pace that the customer can follow. _Understand_ why the customer is calling. _Explain_ in enough detail, and at a pace that the customer can follow. Demonstrate an interested, glad-to-help _Attitude_. Be _Courteous_ and sympathetic, recognizing each customer's particular situation, e.g. death in the family or other tragic circumstances. In later years these five standards were relaxed to three, eliminating Speech and Understanding.

In a remote back room sat an observer of incoming customer calls. This person reported to Dorthea Gale, a manager who was located in the headquarters building. She managed a large team of commercial department "observers" statewide. Her staff was composed of former SRs who had been promoted and trained to observe and record customer call content in a special shorthand. A predetermined number of calls were observed each month in every district. In theory, there was a statistically sound sampling for each manager unit. District managers received monthly reports which included Errors, Irregularities, Slow Attentions, and Tone Breakdowns. These numbers were bashed up against sample sizes, then fitted into pre-determined charts to develop an index. District managers and managers lived and died by this index. When the overall index number dipped below ninety-eight, a variety of corrective actions went into effect. In addition to the Official Observers in the locked back room, there was a Tone Room where supervisors, managers, and district managers could listen to any SR handling calls. Listening-in was an attempt to find individual SRs who were causing the unsatisfactory customer service index. Announcements like "this call may be monitored for training purposes" were non-existent. Privacy law dictating announcements was still years into the future. We listened and acted as we deemed appropriate and necessary for the survival of our business.

My time as a Service Representative came to an end. My initial leadership position arrived. I was to supervise a section that consisted of six positions, each occupied by a Service Representative: Janet Cowan, Ann Cornell, Carol Maulbetch (her brother was a district manager in Traffic), Fran Allen, Joan Hollingsworth, Peggy

Marshall. (She was the daughter of Alberta Peckham, who had been my Initial Training instructor.) Carol Klein was a summer intern from the University of Michigan whose dad, Andy Klein, was district manager in Vinewood, the office where I had almost been initially assigned. At a later date I would work for Mr. Klein in that same district.

It is worth noting that, in this northwest Detroit district, there were about 70 SRs. There was only one minority. Her name was Edna Jett. She was a model SR. She had a Bachelor's Degree (BA) in English from the University of Indiana. One of the goals of the Telephone Company was to do as much business as possible by telephone. However, besides a few pre-written collection letters to send regarding delinquent bills, other letters were occasionally required when customers could not be reached by telephone. In the Webster District, Mrs. Edna Jett wrote all of them. She received requests from SRs or their supervisor on a special form.

She was allowed to close her key, thus shutting off incoming calls, so that she could attend to the needed letter. Her letter-writing skills were exceptional. Edna wrote many letters over many years. The first was 1955.

However, before I was allowed to step into that first supervisory role I had to complete a four-day course in supervision. This course was conducted by Miss Helen O'Conner. The training facility was located on the sixteenth floor of the Michigan Bell headquarters building, 1365 Cass Avenue, in downtown Detroit. We were six newly-appointed supervisors, a group of four from the Detroit area and two from outstate offices. Miss O'Conner was a long-time Commercial department employee. She had begun her career as a clerk, then became a Service Representative, a BOS for many years, and then an instructor charged with the development of newly appointed Business Office Supervisors.

The four days were intense. Helen took us on breaks together; we ate lunch together. It was a departmental chuckle that her students followed behind her like so many chickens, as she led the way to the elevator. No joking allowed.

We each had several "in front of the group" presentations to make. As we were emoting, Helen would be standing aside, looking out the sixteenth floor window. However, do not think that she was not following every word, gesture, and inflection. Her critiques were kind, on the money, frequent, developmental, detailed, and pointed. The four days included company history and structure. The same for AT&T, plus a survey of the twenty-two operating companies besides Michigan Bell. Overviews of Western Electric, the supply arm of the Bell System; Bell Labs; and the Sandia Corporation, which was dedicated to servicing the special communications needs of the Federal Government. The value of Michigan Bell Telephone Company to each local community was stressed. Reasons for each stringent performance standard were reviewed in depth. This was to *insure we understood why we must make it easy to do business by telephone, as calls were our bread and butter.* We began to feel that we were a part of the massive Bell System.

Time spent on the principles of supervision centered on *how to get things done through people without arousing resentment.* We were taught to recognize that errors, irregularities, and lack of proper tone were caused by one or more of the following deficiencies: *lack of knowledge, lack of skill,* or *lack of viewpoint.* Answer the question: "could the performer have done the task properly if her or his life depended on it?" If yes, then training is not the answer. However, more practice might be needed to develop the skill to go with the knowledge already in place. Finally, if the tone was not up to standard, then a bit of attitude adjustment might be required. Helen's students had quite a load to absorb in that four-day session. Many of those basics became their management style for the rest of their careers.

Helen was a Commercial department institution. She lived in a downtown apartment hotel her entire career, walked to work, never owned an auto, and stopped at the very famous St. Aloysius Catholic Church at 1234 Washington Boulevard every morning for a brief prayer. Our class of six agreed that those four days were exemplary, and that we were now ready to lead a section in our various business offices.

Back in the office, I began to supervise the section I had been assigned to even before receiving those four days of supervisor training. The planned three months as a section supervisor went by fast. Those seven young ladies helped me to do well in every way imaginable. Plus, they staged a shower for Ginny, who was pregnant with our first child. They planned this event for an afternoon break, plus one-half hour, agreed to by manager Don Rennick. One of them contacted Ginny to have her arrive as a surprise for me. A cake was baked in the shape of a crib by Janet. There were gifts galore. The major gift, forever memorable, was a beautiful wooden highchair which folded into a work table for use beyond highchair age. It served our family from August 1955 until our youngest grandson was seven years old in February 1997, forty-two years, and still functioning perfectly when we passed it on to Goodwill. That was a delightful introduction to my first managerial position in the Phone Factory, as we often called our employer with affection. My next job would be in the Fort Division office, located in a two-story building at Grand River and Six-Mile Road in Redford, Michigan.

However, before I was transferred I was given an assignment by district manager Morrow. It was Christmastime. I did not have to report to my new assignment until the beginning of the year. He asked me to survey our supervisors and managers to determine what decorations they needed to add to the office Christmas supply. He suggested buying whatever they asked for at the Federal Department Store, directly across the street from our office. He asked if I had cash or credit card to pay for these items. I said yes. He said, "good," and "they are not in our budget so you will have to 'eat them.'" I said "What?" He said, "your manager will explain." Help for my learning curve was not in any manual. My manager explained, "'eat them' means take someone out for a 'business lunch' but don't eat. Then put the 'imagined' lunch on an expense voucher." Michigan State College's school of business had not totally prepared me for the real world of work. The University of Michigan probably did a better job in that regard. I was promoted to Commercial Operations Assistant (COA) and transferred to the Fort Division Office. My days as a college trainee were over. I was now a first-level manager.

☙

COMMERCIAL OPERATIONS ASSISTANT (COA): 1955

In my staff position at the Fort Division office, I reported to a manager duo: Hazen Wilson and Kenneth Young. Amazing to note that Ken had been my family's *Detroit News* paperboy when I was growing up. My dad had forever remembered him as "the best paperboy we ever had." These two managers reported to Jack Eastwood, another U of M grad. There were very few Michigan State grads in the company at that time. That changed substantially over time. Jack reported to Jim Healy, division manager.

The first three months I did projects assigned by my managers, by district supervisor Eastwood, and by Agnes Costello, a BOS. She was responsible for implementation of new methods and procedures throughout the division.

I was fair game to be assigned projects, as I for certain needed to learn the business. These were great experiences.

Then it hit: the real reason for my being there. A new SR sales training package had arrived from AT&T.

All SRs were to receive these new three days of instruction, cleverly named "Package Selling." This simply meant that SRs would suggest or recommend a package of telephone services on all incoming calls for new service. Everyone would be taught to develop facts: the number of rooms, number of levels, and number of persons living in the home. Then a package would be recommended, e.g. wall phone in the basement, bedside extension, second floor extension, always the black wall phone in the attached garage. Monthly expense and installation charges were all added up and quoted using new (complex) handbook pages.

I would report to Al Crumb, district sales manager. I was now on special assignment until the project was complete. He arranged a company car for me: a 1954 black Ford two-door with high mileage. It reeked of smoke from the thousands of cigarettes, cigars, and full pipes of tobacco consumed by salesmen on their way to and from customer premises over the past few years.

I traveled the division, training all management people in each office: Wayne,

Wyandotte, Livonia, Kenwood, Webster, Vinewood, Ann Arbor, Farmington, and Plymouth. It took four months. This was a serious learning experience, especially the need for me to handle a ton of logistics. The "in front of the group" part was easy. The division management team learned to sell packages exactly as the course developers at AT&T had envisioned. They in turn trained the SR force. A lot of packages were sold during the next decade and beyond.

In the summer of 1955, my family and I moved to Royal Oak, Michigan. Driving north on Woodward Avenue between Eleven-Mile Road and Twelve-Mile Road, I discovered a Mobil Oil (Flying Red Horse) gas station. This business was nestled on a small triangular-shaped lot. There were two pumps, regular and premium, plus one bay with a hoist. This turned out to be a father-and-son operation.

My first visit was at random. I needed gas and was passing by. I pulled into the drive. An attendant came out, took my order, pumped the gas, washed the windshield, and wiped off the head lights. As I walked toward the little office with Mobil credit card in hand, I noticed three signs. They had been artfully lettered and covered with clear plastic. The sign over the bay read "Oil

Change & Lube — No Repairs." The sign over the office window read "Hours—6:00 A.M. to 6:00 P.M., Mon. thru Fri., Sat. 6:00 A.M.—12:00 noon, Closed Sunday." It was, however, the sign over the door leading to the office that caught my eye. In the same lettering, with the same plastic covering, it read "we fight poverty; we work." Going forward this was my favorite gas station and a favorite saying.

Standing on the driveway looking north and west across the eight lanes of Woodward Avenue traffic, I viewed the Sinclair gas station location where I had worked away the summer of 1944. The building was gone, but memories of how I had fought poverty that summer eleven years before, remained—I had worked. I had then been sixteen.

෮ඃ

STAFF SUPERVISOR—
METHODS: 1956

My next assignment came about because the district manager in Vinewood asked for me, to fill a recently vacated miscellaneous supervisory position.

I reported to George Feezey for a second time, having had a short time under him in my first office. I thought Andy Kline was asking for me because, having seen me in action training his staff on the new sales package, he thought me an outstanding management person.

Wrong—one of his managers, Bill MacArthur, had been promoted to district manager and was leaving Andy's district. Bill lived in Huntingwoods, not far from his boss Andy, who hated the drive to the Vinewood office, way down Livernois. It was a long uncomfortable commute. With me there, Mr. Kline had a new chauffeur. On Monday mornings he would pick me up at my home in Royal Oak, just a short distance south of his home in Birmingham. I would drive him home at night, and take the auto to my house. Then I would pick him up Tuesday, Wednesday,

Thursday, and Friday mornings, and drive Livernois to 744 West Fort Street. On Friday evenings, we would go to my house. The first time he did that I invited him in to meet my wife and have a beer. He accepted. That "Friday libation" became a tradition for the eight months I worked for Andy. His favorite was Carling Black Label. I bought two cases for the basement, and put a six-pack in the ice box. Andy took the company car home for the weekend, right after his second brew.

Mr. Kline took our Vinewood management group, Nina Peterson, George Fezzey, Jack Chatel, Jim Boury, Bob Healy (division manager's son), and me out for lunch every Friday that he was in the office. Favorite haunts were the Dearborn Inn, Major's (best liver and bacon in town), and Joey Stables. All very nice culinary venues. These luncheons were where plans were laid for the next week and beyond. My tasks included what was recognized in the business as "miscellaneous supervisor." For the several months I was in Vinewood district, I had a different assignment every day. Nothing that I had not done in the almost twelve months I had spent in the Webster district. My learning was just being reinforced.

A memorable event was the renting of space in the Detroit Produce Terminal, directly across the street from the multi-story Vinewood District offices, 740 W. Fort Street. This building housed several telephone company districts, Commercial, Traffic (including two floors of operators), Engineering, and Central Office Switching.

Commercial needed space to train an additional class of SRs. Training supervisor Gloria Heilbrenner, BOS, and I put together a training room next to the area in the Produce Terminal that housed the cabbage, lettuce, and parsnips. On warm days, trainees were provided with a variety of odors to go with their telephone orders and bills.

However, Andy's chauffeur (me) was soon headed for his next assignment: the General Commercial staff in the headquarters building at 1365 Cass Avenue. This nineteen-story building was very impressive, especially in the cathedral-like lobby patterned after AT&T headquarters at 195 Broadway, New York City. My new leader was manager Bob Tripp in the Commercial Methods and Procedures district, led by district manager Gene Lochner.

Assignments were varied and challenging, and there were lots of them. Mr. Tripp was a true methods professional. He was skilled in many areas, and was known for getting things done. He was the first person I heard utter the axiom "*If you want to get something done—ask a busy person.*" We got along fine. His boss, district manager Gene Lochner, lived in Royal Oak. In time, I became a chauffeur once again, but this time using my own auto. I picked Gene up at his home about three miles south of where I lived and drove him to the Bell Building. Not a bad deal, as he paid for our parking in the dirt lot right in back of the office, next to the Grinnell Brothers Music company warehouse. Plus, every so often he would slip me an envelope marked "gas money." Gas in those days, on Woodward Avenue in Royal Oak, was seventeen cents per gallon. In time this dirt parking lot would become an MBT-owned three-story parking garage. Monthly rental for a reserved parking spot would be $15.00.

All men in the Commercial department were invited to attend an annual "Commercial Men's Golf Outing," always on a weekend in mid-June. The year was 1956. This was a weekend affair, which had been a tradition for many years. My first outing had been held at the Saint Clair Inn, on the Saint Clair River in Saint Clair, Michigan, circa twenty-five miles north of Detroit. We often went there for meetings.

The 1956 venue had been changed to the Ramona Park hotel in Harbor Springs, Michigan. This change in venue was to placate the northern Michigan and Upper Peninsula gentleman who said that they were the ones who always had to travel the furthest.

It so happened that I was spending the last three days of the week, before the golf outing in Kalamazoo gathering data for a methods and procedures change. I had driven there on Wednesday with my wife and young son. They were visiting her brother and his family, who lived in Portage, just outside of Kalamazoo. Hence on Friday when I left for Harbor Springs, I had Joe Brogher the Commercial district manager as a passenger. We would travel back to Kalamazoo on Sunday, where I would pick up the family for our return trip to our home in Royal Oak.

These annual golf outings were never defined as to purpose. However, they were put on at considerable corporate expense. Included in the package for every participant were lodging, food and beverages, green fees (for the many golfers), clay pigeons for a few shooters, plus mileage expense ($.07 per mile in those days), and miscellaneous charges. We all assumed that the basic purpose was to develop and maintain camaraderie in the department. Sort of an annual attitude adjustment event.

This outing was a major touchstone for me, not unlike my decision not to accept a commission as a 2nd Lieutenant in the U.S. Army. I was standing chest deep in the swimming pool at the Ramona Park. A man I had met at dinner the evening before swam the length of the pool and stood up next to me leaning against the side of the pool. He was Harry Lawford, division commercial manager for the southern division of Michigan. His office was in Grand Rapids. We talked for a bit about the event, the locale, and the weather. He then said "are you about to be promoted to a second-level manager's position?" I said "I think that is possibly true." He continued "would you be interested in being the manager of the Battle Creek office?"

My worst nightmare was contained in those thirteen words. Battle Creek was wife Ginny's home town. Her dad, Ben Bristol, was a forever member of the Rotary Club. He was a friend of club member Harry Barnes, Michigan Bell Telephone Company manager of the Battle Creek office. Ben had told me on the sly that Harry was about to leave town for a job in a Detroit office. Even though this was a company of circa 30,000 employees, it still boiled down to little segments. Ginny and I had talked about the "what if someday, I was asked to move to Battle Creek to work"? She loved the town. She had been deeply involved all of her life because of her voice, singing in her church choir, soloing for many civic events, and leadership in Campfire Girls. The 1946 Battle Creek Central High School yearbook saluted her with "a smile is currency in any country." However, she was already liking the big city, and all it had to offer: music, art, the Red Wings (her favorite viewer sport), our huge church congregation, a revered minister, a wonderful potluck group. Mostly she wanted to be done with her old home town and just move on. I agreed.

I had only seconds to make the decision. I said "Mr. Lawford, I cannot move to Battle Creek because my wife does not want to go back. I will go happily to Lansing, Grand Rapids, Kalamazoo, Niles, or anywhere else in your domain, just not to 'Cereal City'". Harry was polite in saying that the opening was going to be only in Battle Creek, and he would not be moving any manager other than Harry Barnes. As he swam away, I knew that my opportunity was swimming off alongside him. It would be two more years before a second-level manager's job opened up for me. I knew for certain it would not be in the Southern Division, and it was not. At least this decision did not get me sent to Korea.

Fast forward to June 1957, the last ever "Commercial Men's Golf Outing". The event was back at the Saint Clair Inn, with golf at the Port Huron Golf Club, Fort Gratiot, Michigan for high handicap golfers, and the Black River Country Club, Port Huron, Michigan, for low handicap golfers. Thus endeth those Commercial Men's Golf Outings forever. This apparently was brought about by corporate budget considerations, closer scrutiny by the Public Service (PSC), and possibly more women who did not play golf moving into management positions.

In the spring of 1957, I was involved—along with the entire methods staff—in a trial, billing all Detroit suburban customers via computer. This was a first. We lived all week in Port Huron, working at the accounting center. The computer was an IBM 640. It filled a room 50 x 50 feet, with a massive air conditioning unit to keep it at a proper operating temperature. Input into the computer was via a multitude of eighty-eight-column IBM punch cards, which I seem to remember created a tape for direct input into the 640. We were going along full speed when I put a batch of IBM cards into a sorter upside down. Later a safety feature was added to make this impossible, but it came too late to protect me. The cards got mixed up. It took me one full day to re-file the mess. Today my MacBook Air laptop is far more powerful than that room full of IBM 640 equipment. Thankfully, there are no longer punched cards to sort.

This suburban billing project trial came to a successful conclusion; Detroit suburbs would now receive their telephone bills computed, printed, and mailed from the Port Huron accounting center.

Before I returned to my desk in the Commercial methods district, I was assigned to attend a personnel department management training course. This was properly named IBMC—Interdepartmental Basic Management Course. Unlike the Commercial supervisory course, this experience included relatively new first-level supervisors from all departments: Plant, Traffic, Engineering, Comptroller, Directory, Commercial, and occasionally smaller groups like Public Relations and Personnel.

This week-long course was a live-in experience at the Fort Shelby Hotel on Lafayette Street in downtown Detroit. Twenty attendees, men and women from both local and out-state districts, were enrolled in the course. There were evening sessions to include speakers from a variety of departments. Course instructors were directed by a district manager, a woman named Florence Reiman. Lead instructors were George VanDorne, on loan from the Comptroller's department, and Tom Glavin loaned from the Marketing department. Instructional methods were varied. However, solving problems was definitely one major theme. The training situations were not the Harvard Business School cases, but were similar, geared to help new supervisors understand how to deal with a multitude of "things" coming at us all at once. Great stuff; and a feeling among all of us that if the Company was willing to spend the money to house and feed us, take us off the job for a whole week, and have "high level officials" work with us in the evening, this training, our jobs, and *we* must be pretty important. There were other management training and education courses to consider as one moved along in the business. Little did I know, in this early stage of my career, that one day I would be the director of that training and educational operation. Sadly, not long after our weeklong session ended, Florence was driving across a railroad track on Jefferson Avenue on her way to work when she was hit by a train and killed.

(Note: In my opinion, the reason Michigan Bell Telephone was able to promote almost exclusively from within, was because of the basic and continuation management training and education provided to managers at the first two levels.)

My last methods and procedures assignment was part of a nationwide AT&T study of Business Office Supervisor productivity. The purpose was to determine if supervisors were spending their time in the most effective manner possible. Two persons were assigned to a task force reporting to me: Marge O'Connor from the general training staff, and Vivian Bischoff from the commercial observing staff. We travelled the State. We were observing BOS employees in many different offices, recording their every move for every minute of the day. We, of course, chuckled, saying the only break we got was when our subjects went to the bathroom. That was true. We had to plan to go at the same time, so they did not get to do any work that did not get recorded.

The quantity of data, before being summarized, filled many large storage boxes. When summarized, it filled a fat binder. We each had a box full of cataloged 3x5 cards in summary mode. My first out-of-town trip for my new company was to New York with Al Lewis, division level manager and director of Commercial Methods, Training, and Results. We were meeting with our counterparts from the other twenty-two Bell operating companies. The AT&T methods and procedures vice president and his staff ran the meeting. Company representatives presented summaries of their findings. Two days were then spent putting it all together, summarizing discoveries, and developing recommendations to share with every operating company.

It all worked out. A heady experience. Al Lewis was a real mentor. He knew New York City well. We had dinner in Greenwich Village at the Penguin, a high-end eatery. The watercress salad cost $4.50, a fortune in 1957. We went to a bar where waiters and waitresses all sang opera as they worked. There was a handheld microphone on an overhead wire. They passed it back and forth. Al ordered a bottle of Miller High Life. Me too. It was $1.00 per bottle. We sat at the bar. The bartender was the Basso. We each had two beers.

Al paid with a $5.00 bill, tipping $1.00. That was sixty years ago. I was impressed. As we sat at the bar, I remembered that I had forgotten my "Dopp" kit, with shaving stuff, tooth brush, etc. I mentioned this to Al. "No problem, we will stop at the drugstore on the way to the hotel. Buy whatever you need, a new carrier if needed. Be sure to put it all on your expense voucher when you fill it out. Save the receipts." This was another lesson not written in any training material, something like "eating Christmas decorations."

Al and I made one final stop in Greenwich Village to visit Whit Jones. He was living there on a three-year rotational assignment with AT&T. We met his new fiancée Ann. We had a cup of coffee. (Note: Mr. Jones was the only second-level manager I ever knew about who was loaned to AT&T, promoted to third-level district manager going to New York, and promoted to fourth-level division manager coming back to Michigan Bell.)

I must have been deemed ready; because on return from N.Y., I was promoted to the coveted "L" level position as a second-level Manager. My first managerial assignment was in the Order Unit of the Trinity District, 105 East Bethune, across the street from the Detroit Police Department's well-respected mounted division. The horses did not seem to notice that I had arrived.

଎

In June 1959 I had graduated from the University of Detroit, evening division, with a Masters of Business Administration (MBA) degree. I had begun this adventure in the fall of 1955, taking one-half of a graduate load of four credits each semester. Total credits required for the degree were thirty. The cost per credit hour was $16.00. I had used the GI Bill.

A situation had developed in January which required another bout of serious decision making. I was taking a graduate course in economics with a focus on labor issues. The adjunct instructor was a Ph.D. from the University of Indiana, Bloomington, Indiana. His name is lost in time. He was on sabbatical working for the U.S. Government as an arbitrator between Great Lakes Steel and the United Steelworkers Union. He said he was teaching "to keep current for his return to the university classroom the next year."

As the semester moved on he asked me if I would be willing to teach his one undergraduate class should he be tied up in a late-evening negotiation. I said "Yes. How would I get your notes?" Not to worry, he gave me duplicates of his notes for the six remaining sessions. I received a late call twice and did it. The semester ended. I graduated. The professor set up a time when he could visit me at home and settle up. He gave me a check for $50.00. He also brought me a fifth of Old Grandad whiskey. I thanked him and put it in the cupboard. Someone told me later that I should have offered him a drink and joined him. Learning the ways of the world took time. I was thirty-one.

What he really brought was an offer to clear the way for me to become a Ph.D. candidate in Business Management at the University of Indiana.

This included inexpensive faculty housing, a tuition scholarship, and a full-time teaching fellow (TF) position. He advised that I would need some supplemental income for the two-year program, such as loans or family assistance. This was quite an honor. No rush. He was leaving for home in mid-July. Take a look at it, and let him know by then.

Ginny and I had a brief moment of seeing those ivy-covered halls at the end of the two years, with doctorate in hand. We didn't go to Bloomington. I had just been promoted to a second-level manager's position, had two sons ages four and two, and a new house. We passed on the opportunity. I liked the telephone business, so far, and the people who worked there. It was a very tempting offer, but in our judgment, just not doable at that moment in time. We never looked back.

☙

ORDER MANAGER—TRINITY: 1959

Hired as a College Trainee (CT). Promoted to a first-level management position as a Commercial Operations Assistant (COA). And now, five years into my career, promoted to a second-level position as a Business Office Manager ("L" Level) in a City location, the Trinity District, Woodward Division.

Arriving early on that first morning. I located an attended parking lot one block away from the ten-story Bell Building at 105 East Bethune. This building housed central office equipment, plus operators, engineers, and sales personnel. The Commercial Office took up an entire floor, the tenth. The size was a tad smaller than the Webster office where I had started. My desk was in a corner on an angle overlooking the SR positions. The office in total appeared about the same as what I was used to, with one major exception.

During the time I was moving from assignment to assignment in the Fort Division and on the general staff, the entire Commercial

Department had undergone an operational restructuring. This change was named "the Roseville Plan." The name stuck because that is where the "plan" was initially designed, developed, and implemented. Roseville district manager John Birkhold guided the trial to great success. Later on, I would work as a manager in his district. John and his wife, Gretchen, and my wife, Ginny, and I, had been members of the Royal Oak First Presbyterian Church for many years.

The plan, which was already up and running in my new office, involved customer service and billing records. They were no longer filed together. Orders were now in one unit, and bills were in another unit. Incoming customer calls were screened by the operator as to "is this about your bill?" If no, the call was directed to the Order unit, otherwise to the Billing Unit. The call was thus being directed to a "specialist" in Services or Billing. (Note: The term Billing was really a misnomer. It should have been called "Collections," as that was the true function of the group.)

This change had required tremendous effort in every office statewide. It had been in the planning stage for quite some time. Two things drove the effort. First, Service Representative training expense was increasing with increased service and equipment offerings, and bills were becoming more complex. Training a new SR was taking eight weeks. By separating Orders and Bills, SR training was reduced to four weeks for an order SR to become productive, and to three weeks for a Billing SR. Force losses were in the 20% to 25% range, hence turnover required a steady flow of trainees coming out of initial training. Second, with the newly introduced package selling, there were now order experts who did not need to be concerned with billing matters. Sales took off. I was the Order Manager. Across the office was Dave Ryckman, the Billing Manager.

The Order Unit contained twelve positions: two Sections of six SRs each, with a supervisor for each section, Madonna Campbell and Mary Margaret McKendry. The Order Room (teletyping) was supervised by Betty Baker. There was a four-position business group supervised by Mary Tata. This group took care of business customers not large enough to warrant a salesman's telephone call or visit. Barbara Kehn was the relief supervisor.

I would report to Jaxon Wysong, district manager. I arrived early that first morning. He arrived and welcomed me heartily, and gave me a list he had personally typed. It was headed *"Exposers" for Mr. Vahlbusch*. We followed this sequence for the next three days. Included in these exposures were several long sessions observing (listening) to SRs handling incoming customer calls. One thing Mr. Wysong was dead set against was when an SR recommended a package containing a one-party line, extension telephones, all in color, and then sometimes tried to sneak an additional listing at $.35 per month into the package. There had been some accusations in the past that this was being done to raise the monthly revenue in the district. In fact, Jaxon said that he was "diabolically" opposed to that practice. I almost said *"the devil you are,"* but I refrained. We got along fine. I had to be certain to listen carefully to whatever Mr. Wysong said, as his choice of words was on occasion confusing, at least to me as a new manager.

Mr. Wysong's secretary, Ruth Gustafson, was most helpful. She knew where to find files and records, and understood the nuances of all those District and Division reports. She also had the inside track for rumors, which usually turned out to be true. First rumor she shared was that, after Jaxon attended his daughter's wedding in Texas, he would be transferring to the Division office. He and his wife were taking the train to Texas. This daughter was his from a previous marriage. He had shown me several photos of his relatively new wife. She was pretty. Ruth also said that the Division rumor mill had a Mr. Thomas Fezzey moving into the Trinity District job. All these rumors came true. Mr. Wysong was back in his office for one week. He showed me several photos of himself and his wife on the train, even one in the upper bunk of their roomette. Amazing. Quite a man. He wore either yellow or pink socks every day.

Business Office managers had a unique position in the company. This department grew with the growth of the telephone business in general. In the beginning, if a customer wanted to order a telephone or move a telephone, they called the installation department. For a question on their bill they called the accounting department. If a telephone repair was needed, the repair department. Hence, the commercial department was developed so the customer or potential customer could get it all done with one call. Employees in the commercial department thus became advocates for the customer. It worked very well, as long as management people in commercial did not start feeling too inspired by their "power." One example from my first manager's position explains it all. What a learning experience it turned out to be.

An SR received a call from a customer who claimed that the installer who came out to her home to install new service refused to complete the job. SR referred the call to her supervisor, since she was not certain what to do. The supervisor talked with her counterpart in the installation department, and was unable to get a commitment to make the installation the next day.

I received the complaint. I called my counterpart in the installation department, Len Weil (he had begun his career installing telephones in this very area riding a Michigan Bell bicycle). I told Len that they had to get this telephone installed today. It was not yet 10:00 A.M. What a man. He would soon turn out to be forever in my "best friend" category. However, it took a little while. He said, "meet me in the Company lot next door. We will drive out and meet the installer and his supervisor at the customer's premises." We did. We entered the home and met the lady of the house. Len said to me, "Russ, why don't you check out the basement;

see if you can locate the connection box." No problem for a newly promoted commercial manager eager to learn. When I got to the top step going down into the basement, I saw that there were at least two feet of water with raw sewage floating across the entire basement floor. I was in shock. Embarrassed, I gave the lady of the house one of my newly printed cards, showing that I was the "Manager." I said to her, "the minute you have your basement drained, scrubbed with a disinfectant, and it is bone dry, call me on my direct line. I will have your service installed within 24 hours." We left.

The four of us stood at the curb, next to an olive-drab company truck, a supervisor's two-door black Ford, and a manager's two-door black Chevrolet. I took the lead, asking if we could all meet for lunch at the Terova Rathskeller on John-R Street. This was an above-average vintage German restaurant. I said, "let's not plan to go back to the office after lunch." Yes, the installation supervisor would sign the installer out and get the line-dispatcher to reassign his afternoon appointments. We met. We each had two 20 oz. drafts of Dortmunder German beer. We had a huge lunch, including top-of-the-line bratwurst. We ate slowly, and I said that it was a shame they did not feature "crow" on the menu for me. That lesson stood me in good stead on that day, and for thirty more years.

Our new district manager Tom Fezzey arrived. First thing, he invited me to the cafeteria for morning coffee and planning. We got our coffee and went to a nearby table. I sat on the side, Tom at the head of the table. As he sat down he tipped the full cup of the hot stuff into his lap. He showed the calmness he displayed in future crisis situations. He said, "Russ, would you please go to my office and bring me my topcoat. I will be going to my cleaners in Allen Park, then home." He looked at his watch, adding, "meet me here for lunch at 12:30 P.M. and we will have our meeting." I did. We did. We got along famously. We had some success with the indexes. We got into some difficulty from time to time, and worked out of those negative situations. Sales results were excellent month after month. Division manager Jim Richards held Tom in high esteem. Jim visited us often, always with a motto to spur us to greater heights. One of his favorites, having to do with our discussions regarding how to run the business office, was this: *"If we agree on everything, one of us is unnecessary."* Jim was an early riser. He frequently was in the office when I arrived, and my TOA was circa 7:30 A.M. He had ideas ready. He was so intense he occasionally forgot to shave his upper lip. I would ask him if he was growing a mustache. His response was always the same, "oh damn, I was thinking about..." and he would name some new idea, and off we would go on an in-depth discussion. He was a hands-on leader with the management staff even two levels below him (me). This included long lunches each quarter with each manager. Very unusual. Very enjoyable. Very informative. This drove some of his district managers crazy.

It was just over one year later when district manager Fezzey was promoted to Division level and moved to a new job. Division Manager Richards was also transferred. Where these new positions were located is lost in the ether. District Manager Frank Phillips was transferred from Royal Oak commercial to Trinity commercial. I did not know Frank Philips. However, district secretary Ruth Gustafson had the skinny on him from her counterpart in Royal Oak. Here is what she related.

Mr. Phillips was a very experienced district Commercial Manager. He is said to say of himself that he is *"firm, friendly, and fair.* He tells it like it is. He expects the best from all his management people all the time." Ruth's research turned out to be right. I got along fine with Frank. Our results were acceptable. Never great. We did have some fantastic months. He had a meeting each month when results charts arrived. His admonition after an especially good month was always the same *"nothing is as old as yesterday's results; now let's all get back to work."* We did.

After I had worked for Frank for just under one year, he called me into his office one afternoon. What he said to me changed many things. "Russ, you have a good mind. You have very creative ideas. *Your skill at presenting these ideas needs a lot of work.* I will give you the same advice my father (a Presbyterian minister) gave me. Take the Dale Carnegie Course." I did.

I had to borrow the tuition ($250.00) from the Telephone Employees Credit Union. Reimbursement from the Company education assistance program came only after I had received my successful completion certificate. Frank was right. When I completed the fourteen sessions, I was selected to be an unpaid "graduate assistant." In time this led to an opportunity to be one of 1,700 instructors worldwide. My first and longest moonlighting endeavor. Over time that experience helped me move into my dream job in

Personnel: Management Training and Education. More on the Dale Carnegie Course later.

The majority of SRs in the Trinity district, which was located just north of Grand Boulevard and just off Woodward Avenue in mid-town Detroit, came from the north: Royal Oak, Berkley, Ferndale, occasionally Birmingham. I lived in Royal Oak. Hence when the Suburban Bus Company drivers went on strike in 1960, I transported SRs to and from the office. I collected Carmen Silva, Julie Sebolka, Andrea Sebolka, Kay Kinsinger, and Happy Burke, and whisked them to and from the Trinity building so we did not have to close up shop. Fortunately, the bus driver work stoppage only lasted for six working days.

Managing a Business Office Unit was interesting, challenging, and rewarding.

I was responsible for the entire package: planning, organizing, directing, controlling, training, motivating, and supervising. Turnover was constant, so hiring and training had to match losses. Working with a recruiter in Trinity, Ms. Athalee Dyer, we found the necessary number of new hires to go into training for the number of weeks required to get them ready to handle those incoming customer calls, billing, and orders. The employee base produced those acceptable numerical results with guidance from their supervisors. The manager was supposed to make it all run smoothly by not interfering too much.

One note about recruiting. Applicants came from newspaper advertisements, high school yearbook ads, and walk-ins into public offices. However, most arrived as the result of referrals from other employees. Often entire families worked for MBT. Our Trinity recruiter would review the paperwork from an applicant, administer the IQ test (Army Alpha), determine that she had a prospect, then conduct an interview. If all went well, there was one final step: the home visit. The purpose was to talk with parents to try to determine if they were supportive of their daughter accepting this job, and to get a feel as to whether they planned to stay in the area for at least two years. The two years was also a question asked of the applicant, "Will you agree to spend at least two years on this job?" What a joke. I talked with women who had worked for the Company for a multitude of years (up to fifty) and they all said that when they were asked this question they lied, because they had either no intention of staying for two years, or they had no idea how long they would be there. Occasionally the home visit was with a husband or live-in friend. Most applicants were women under twenty years of age. The idea was to try to determine if he thought it a good match at MBT, and to get a feel as to how long they might be living in the area. Some of the findings from home visits were quite amazing, and did in fact uncover information which caused some job offers not to be made. If it all looked good, a job offer was tendered.

Because the number of telephone customer calls was so vast, situations often arose that required special managerial attention. On occasion these situations offered a bit of comic relief.

SR turns a call over to her supervisor, because she did not know what to do. Customer tells the supervisor that she was at work when the telephone man came to her home to install an extension. The apartment manager, as prescribed by Michigan Bell, had gone with the installer to the apartment. Manager had to leave for some reason. When the customer arrived home the extension was in, her parakeet was missing, and the toilet seat was up. That meant to the customer that the installer had flushed the bird down the toilet. Bob Walters worked in the district as an Outside Representative. He made calls on customers when no other solution worked, by telephone or mail. Bob visited the upset parakeet owner. He reported that he "calmed the lady down." Looked around the apartment; in time locating the little bird hanging helplessly high up on the window side of the drapes, with a claw caught in the fabric. Customer satisfied. Just another day in the Phone business.

One more example: in this case representing cooperation with a fellow manager. Dave Ryckman was the billing manager. He called me just before 5:00 P.M., asking if I would stay around for a bit, as he had an appointment at 5:15 P.M. with a customer, and was not comfortable being alone with this gentleman. The customer arrived and was buzzed into the office. He was very big, very muscular. His announced name was "Race Horse Smith."

He had with him a crosscut saw, hanging from his belt. He also had a full tool box. He explained that he was a finish carpenter. He had lost his driver's license and was taking the bus to jobs. He had come to pay a deposit in order to get four Princess telephones installed for his four nieces at his home. Checking the records, he did have an order placed as stated, and the deposit had been requested, $30.00 per line. Mr. Smith pulled out a large roll of bills and paid the freight. Dave wrote out a receipt. We shook hands all around. Race Horse left.

I set up an auditor's investigation as to how "Race Horse" got approved as a white-pages directory listing. The audit was helped along by a brief article in the Detroit News a week later. It read: "a gentleman named Mr. Race Horse Smith has been accused of jumping the meter on his Detroit Edison electric service, resulting in his neighbor being billed for his electricity usage. Edison has rewired these services to correct the situation." It concluded with, "a substantial deposit has been requested to be paid before the customer's electric service will be restored." Mr. Smith's name was changed in the next white pages telephone directory, using a first name I cannot remember. Probably "John." Just another day at Ma Bell.

Business office managers were responsible for planning, organizing, directing, controlling, training, and motivating, plus supervising a staff of supervisors (usually three to six), who in turn supervised six to eight SRs.

Planning included estimating the number of incoming calls for each hour of each work day. Then estimating and assigning the correct number of Service Reps to answer these calls from customers. Obviously, months differed as to number of work days, either 157.5 hours, or 165.0 hours. (February was of course a special case). Below the Eight-Mile Road 7.5 hour days; above the Eight-Mile Road 8.0 hour days. So, in the suburbs and out-state those numbers changed to 168.0 and 176.0. Each month had either 21 or 22 work days. Telephone Company business offices were not open on Saturday or Sunday.

Incoming call data from past years was available on spreadsheets. These data were for the most part stroke records, difficult to locate and to read.

Current call volumes were available and were the best source adjusted as to the date and day of the month. Mondays and days after holidays were always the busiest, as Ma and Pa had talked about their telephone service when they were both at home. Then they had to get that call in on Monday, often in the morning. Very busy time.

When I was being taught by my first boss, Earl Morrow, to do force requirement estimating, he handed me a slide rule to convert call volumes to employee equivalents based on estimated call volumes by hour. I was amazed that this was the computation tool of choice. Not to worry, I had taken a one-credit, one-day-per-week slide-rule course at 7:00 A.M. in the lower level of my dorm at Michigan State, just because I was curious when my engineering school roommate sat for hours sliding that "thing" back and forth. Luck is important as careers unfold.

In addition to all of the fundamental duties of the manager, there were always those out-of-the-blue moments at which complex problems needed to be solved. More than one of my district managers said that "this was why I was being paid that big money." Then they always laughed. Me too.

I had been a manager for about six weeks when one of my supervisors referred a problem situation to me. It had come to her from one of her SRs. The recently released annual white pages had a compilation problem. The directory showed that Basinger Tire Company, a very large tire dealer located on Woodward Avenue in our district, had one of its main telephone numbers incorrectly listed as a number belonging to Bart's Tavern on the lower Eastside of Detroit. This meant that if a potential tire customer looked up Basinger in the white pages, they would retrieve a number, that would actually reach Bart's. I was certain Bart did not want Tire calls. I was even more certain that the tire company did not want to lose a potential customer to Bart. I was new, but I knew this was bad. BAR-BAS, it could and did happen.

What to do? I called the Michigan Bell Law Department. A law clerk answered. I had come to the right place. She was the one who assigned attorneys to cases. She assigned their newest attorney, Miss Mary Petey (a.k.a. Conrad).

Mary was the first MBT female attorney. Miss Petey would call me. She did.

We met and devised a strategy. Set up an appointment with Bart for the next afternoon at 2:00 P.M. A memorable meeting. We learned a lot.

As we sat at the bar drinking 7-Up, Bart stood behind it and talked. Quite a long discussion. Our position was that Bart should give up the telephone number to the tire company. We would give him a new number. He would assess how this had hurt his business, and we would take that dollar figure to our top management for approval.

Now it is our turn to listen and learn. Bart had one telephone number, but he had two telephones, one at each end of the bar. One was an extension, both of which according to code had to be within visual distance of each other. This was to prevent someone listening without the originator or receiver of the call being aware that someone else was on the line. This set up, Bart explained in detail, was because, having been in business for twenty years, he had many "regulars." If he gave up this telephone number it would all but ruin his business. He had many married men and women who used his establishment as their "second home." They met their "significant others" at Bart's. They called them from Bart's. Plus, they received calls on that number explaining why they could not meet on a particular day or night. Attorney Petey and I talked it over. We offered Bart the only other possible solution. This was no fault of his; it was ours. We needed to solve it now.

With his agreement we would arrange what was known as a "double intercept." Anyone who called the tire company telephone number, which was really the bar number, would reach a special operator, and visa versa. The operator would have a list, and would know to ask the caller "whom do you want to reach?" If the answer was Bart's Bar, they would be connected to the two telephones at the ends of the bar. If the answer was Tire Company or Basinger's, they would be connected to an alternate number at the tire company. This error would be corrected in the next white pages in April.

Miss Petey and I set up an appointment with the Basinger Tire Company communications director for the next morning. The manager was not thrilled, but realizing that was the only possible solution without law suits or a huge payoff to Bart, agreed. Being in the communications part of the tire business, the manager also realized that "double intercept" was very costly for the telephone company to put into effect 24/7/365. However, we deserved it for the error.

Mary and I were both new to our positions. We felt pretty good about having put this mess to bed. Fast forward: she does very well in the Law Department. She marries fellow attorney Al Waterstone. She becomes the first woman in the Company to be promoted to Assistant Vice President.

Many others followed. In fact, into the future I would report to two different women AVPs, plus a division manager.

But back to Mary (then Mrs. Waterstone). Each year the Company President—Dave Easlick at that time—hosted a black-tie dinner for all AVP-level and above management personnel. A very posh affair. It was tradition at the end of the evening for wives of these high-level officials to receive a piece of Steuben glass. Very beautiful. Very expensive. Even back then nothing under $200.00. The glass company had been founded in 1903. This particular glass was named for the New York county in which the manufacturer, Corning Glass Works, was located.

AVP Mary Waterstone takes her spouse to his, and her, first black-tie affair. Al receives his first piece of Steuben glass, shape and size unknown, right along with all other spouses. The next year, the invitation arrives in the Waterstone household for their second black-tie affair. As Mary told it, Al says over breakfast, "Can I (not may I) please have an end-of-evening gift other than a chunk of glass?" Mary's answer was, "I do not know, but I will check with the Activities supervisor, Lee Stevens, in the Conference Bureau. What shall I tell her you would prefer?"

Al was an avid golfer. His answer was a new Ping putter. He even told her the model number. These prized clubs were in the Steuben glass price range of about $200. Mary checked with Lee. Lee checked with President Easlick. Lee claimed that Dave laughed so hard she was caught up in it all and laughed right along with him. Lots of things going on as women began to become involved in high-level positions of leadership. Al received his Ping putter amid a flurry of congratulations from his fellow spouses.

As I look back at these wonderful times of learning to manage, hopefully more and more effectively, I recall an early program on television named "The Naked City" (1958-1963), obviously intended to be or represent New York without saying so. At the end of each program a deep male voice intoned: "There are seven million stories in the Naked City; this has been one of them."

I borrowed that thought and paraphrased it: "there are millions of stories in a Michigan Bell Telephone Company career; here are but a few of them."

When it was announced that a manager was being transferred, it was often a bit of a poignant moment. One did bond with the team over two or three years.

I had that kind of a moment when I left that first manager's position in the Trinity District. My next position moved me to the Woodward Division office. In this assignment I would report first to Jaxon Wysong (once again), then to Jim Coates (just back from a two-year rotation at AT&T, now a Division Manager). I had followed him into the Trinity order manager's job. The last time I had seen Jim was over two years before. He was battling the Corporate transfer group to get them to pay to have his sailboat moved to New Jersey, since he was being transferred to his new job at AT&T in New York. They finally paid. Then I reported, for the third time, to George Fezzey. This was a special assignment, using newly prescribed seminar materials strongly recommended by AT&T.

George Fezzey and I began preparations for delivering this three-day seminar to each commercial district team in the Woodward Division, which included Royal Oak, Pontiac, Townsend, Trinity, Woodward. With the help of the Corporate Conference Bureau, namely Lee Stevens, we selected a top-flight venue: the Rackham Building, on Farnsworth and Woodward Avenue in mid-town Detroit. Menus were selected for each luncheon, ending up on the last day with a N.Y. Strip, and a baked potato with fancy garnishes.

The seminar included a host of discussion topics. Overall there were three primary purposes.

1. Bring management employees on board about the effectiveness of Package selling of

services and instruments to residential customers.

Results from all twenty-three operating companies in the Bell System were to be reviewed. Discussion of how this additional sales effort was affecting business office operations.

2. Introduce thoughts about the local telephone company being referred to as a "monopoly." The consent decree was still more than twenty-five years away. The purpose here was to show that we were a "natural monopoly," necessary if we were to avoid duplication of poles, switches, plus a multitude of other functions, all raising costs to the consumer. We also discussed the fact that the Bell System was in competition for goods and services, competing for the best employees and having to pay competitive prices on the open market for millions of conductor feet of lead-sheathed copper.

I had a close-to-home example of "natural monopoly." My paternal grandfather owned and operated an interior decorator business in Detroit, before the *natural telephone monopoly* took hold. He was forced to have telephone service from two companies: Home Telephone and Michigan Bell. He wanted to decorate people's homes, no matter which telephone company they utilized.

3. Roll out the Bell System's announcement of changes in the manner of selecting and developing top-level managers. The traditional way was to hire college grads and put them through training that provided them with knowledge about the jobs they would be supervising and managing, plus give them staff experiences in a variety of areas. The updated method was to hire college graduates, but only the top academic performers, plus to recruit class officers and fraternity and sorority officers. This revision fit in with the long-existing Bell policy of promoting from within. This new program was named Interdepartmental Management Development Program (IMDP). The plan was this: immediately place the newly hired IMDP into a second-level management position in any department. Set challenging criteria and goals. Conduct a major performance evaluation at the end of the year, and decide "keeper" or "no keeper." High risk; high reward. Many IMDP's were retained. Some left by invitation; some of their own accord.

Introducing this major management development change fostered much discussion at this seminar. It was in part quite controversial. I remember long-time district manager Otto Bauer, at that time in the Royal Oak District, sitting at the head of the long table in the Rackham conference room. He was smoking his antique Meerschaum pipe (many persons smoked something at conferences in those days). Otto opined in his big voice; "those IM—Drips" are going to go up the ladder of success, wrong, by wrong, by wrong." Over time this leadership development plan did very well, producing a fine batch of leaders for Division level and above positions. Our seminar received high marks.

After I was named to replace Jim Coates as manager of the Trinity district order unit, he offered to show me the ropes. We set up a morning just prior to his leaving for the two-to-three-year rotational assignment at AT&T in New York City. He was very thorough in making certain I had an understanding of the strengths and weaknesses of the order unit at that moment in time. This was all very helpful, even though it was immediately obvious to me that much changed almost every day. That is what managers are paid to do — manage change.

However, there was one non-office related incident that remains in my memory bank. Jim and I were standing in the company cafeteria line on the 3rd floor. Jim stepped in back of me, turned me around and introduced me to a young man. His name was Don Frayer. Jim said two things: 1) "Russ, it is very unusual to find three Michigan State College graduates together at Michigan Bell." 2) "Take heed of Mr. Frayer; he is one of the new IMDP's. We will all be working for him in the not too distant future". Jim's assessment turned out to be an accurate one.

The rumor mill had me moving to yet a third Division, Gratiot, for another learning experience. This time in a suburban office. Roseville, Eleven-Mile Road and Gratiot, was to be my first billing unit experience reporting to district manager John Birkhold. The rumor mill was right once again. I was transferred.

☙

BILLING/ORDER MANAGER— ROSEVILLE: 1962

The Michigan Bell Roseville District office was located at Eleven-Mile Road and Gratiot Avenue in the city of Roseville. It was a two-story yellow brick building.

The record office was on the second floor. The ground floor contained a public office, training rooms, offices for Commercial, Plant, and Traffic district managers. Storage facilities and restrooms completed the ground floor. There was no basement.

This office was north of Eight-Mile Road and hence was a 40-hour office.

Starting time was 8:00 A.M., not 8:30 A.M. like it had always been for me before, having worked in Detroit where the work week was 37.5 hours. Another interesting difference was that the salary scale was lower in suburban offices, by about 6%. When a management person was transferred it usually made no difference, unless you were at the top of the City pay scale. Then you would be "redlined" with no increases until your salary matched the lower top pay. The reason for this was never clear to me, but apparently had something to do with longer commutes to the city, with the accompanying added travel and parking expenses. Hence, we were paid more for fewer hours of work. For managers it made little difference as everyone I knew spent more hours than those minimums getting the job done.

Conversion to the Roseville Plan had been completed about two years previously. It was, after all, the trial district. My assignment was to manage the Billing Unit. There were two Sections, one supervised by Ginny Monte, the other by Kay McDougall. Rita Thompson was training and public office supervisor. Beverly Miller was the relief supervisor. She also did initial training of SRs for both the billing and order units.

The work was quite uniform, from one office to another. The Billing Unit in this district ran well. Collections in the suburban areas were easier than in the city, although there were a small number of affluent customers who were slow payers, often having sizable bills. All the supervisors were experienced and very competent. As long as the manager (me) did not get in their way, things went smashingly. District Manager Birkhold often stated, *"Managing is teaching."*

John had put the "Roseville Plan" together and had helped guide it to success company-wide. He ran a very successful district. He never called anyone by name, always either "fella" or "gal." He sometimes seemed not to be listening, but that was not true. He was always listening, never forgetting anything you had said.

When John took a manager out for lunch, usually for a planning session or annually for an appraisal review, he always selected the Big Boy. He usually ate a "Slim Jim." I played the game and did the same. Very tasty.

One of his early managers had been George Voorhees, who ran the Centerline Office. As that office was closing, George became part of the Roseville Plan implementation team. He loved to tell a story about his boss John Birkhold. Michigan Bell Telephone Company's supplier of choice was Western Electric. For some reason, when old-fashioned wooden rulers were ordered, Western only stocked and sent 18" rulers, not the standard 12" model. As the story goes, John was measuring the office space to determine placement of desks within the new layout, separating order and billing positions. Ruler in hand, John scissor-stepped his way across the office, holding the ruler horizontally and counting the number of feet. He reached the windowed wall overlooking Gratiot Avenue, checking George's desk layout chart.

Using John's final measurements, several desks would be located in the middle of Gratiot Avenue. He called George to his office to inform him that there was not enough room for the desks as laid out on his chart. According to George's remembrance, he was still holding the 18" ruler in his hand like an old-time schoolmarm. George, as tactfully as possible, explained to his leader that for every step he had taken he had lost 6" of desk space. That story had legs. When John retired it was a highlight at his goodbye dinner. One gag gift was a 12" ruler from Kresge's Dime Store.

Another opportunity awaited me in this assignment in a suburban office. Managers statewide were "encouraged" to join a service club—Lions, Exchange, Rotary, Kiwanis. I never considered myself a joiner. However, I was assigned to become a member of the St. Clair Shores Kiwanis club. There were two clubs, one at noon and one at 6:30 P.M. I requested membership in the noon version, as I lived in Royal Oak circa twenty miles west of St. Clair Shores. Request granted. This particular Kiwanis group had a majority of school officials: the superintendent of schools, high school principal, two junior-high principals. Beyond this education group were two dentists, one car-rental manager, one well-known TV personality (Jac LeGoff), a florist, and some other representatives from community businesses.

The monthly luncheon was served at a bowling alley with a kitchen. A group of ladies from the Saint Clair Shores neighborhood put on a nice spread for us. We paid well. Those Kiwanians did good work. Youth was the focus. Both dentists did pro bono work on young folks in need. Kiwanis paid for any materials used in procedures. Other good works were the rule. In my experience, the day you join a service club you are put in line to one day become an officer, up to and including the presidency. I was careful not to get in that line for upward mobility. This was because I knew that my tenure in that area was somewhat limited. As an elected officer, I would be bound to spend a year travelling back and forth from my next assignment. Even so, I was an enthusiastic Kiwanian. One of the years I sold more peanuts than any member. The truth is, I did not sell on street corners that year, but rather purchased a supply of three boxes of peanuts (fifty count each) to hand out at the door on Halloween. The little goblins loved them.

The Roseville district personnel changed. Don Larson, the Order Manager, was moved to the General Commercial Staff to rewrite portions of the massive Business Office Practices binder. Don was very knowledgeable in both the Practices and Procedures arenas. He left Roseville. I left Billing and moved across the office to Orders. A newly hired IMDP (Peter Vandergutch) moved into the Roseville billing unit. The district continued to function. Peter was a good man. He was Dutch (like his boss/mentor Mr. Birkhold). He was a graduate of Calvin College in Grand Rapids, Michigan. His religion was Dutch Reformed. When he arrived he stated that he was not allowed to work on Sunday. When his boss asked him to ride in a Saint Clair Shores parade on a Sunday, in a Michigan Bell rented convertible with logos pasted on the side, they got into a heavy discussion. I was not privy to what occurred. All I know is that the next time I talked to Peter, he was calling from his new office in Grand Rapids. He was now the assistant registrar at his Alma Mater. It was a Wednesday afternoon. He admitted to picking that time to bug me because he had just gotten back from playing nine holes of golf with the president of the college and two other colleagues. This was, according to Peter, a weekly happening during the warm months. In time he became the Registrar. Dick Strauss replaced Peter as Billing Manager.

As I returned from lunch at about 1:40 p.m. EST, on November 22, 1963, order room supervisor Marge Heisner approached me looking very distressed. She relayed the news that President Kennedy had been shot, and was on the way to a Dallas, Texas, hospital. No need to describe my personal feelings regarding that tragedy. The business situation does however warrant a bit of review.

Calls into the business office ceased. SRs were sitting quietly. Phones were silent. It was just as well that no calls were arriving, because I do not believe any of us would have been able to deal with them. However, the central office was beyond buzzing; it was frozen. The number of customers attempting to make calls was so voluminous that only a very few were able to get through. In essence the switching gear was inoperative, and stayed that way for several hours.

When it became apparent that no business would get done, we decided to send two thirds of the SR force home. We surveyed everyone. A large group left. Those remaining had a one-half-day-off credit into the future.

I was unable to get a call through to my wife. The office did not own a radio, so I spent a few minutes listening to the details on our car radio. Never before, and never again, did business offices stop functioning in just a few seconds.

The district expanded. Reason? The Mount Clemens office, the entire HO-ward exchange, moved into our office. Using a 50' retractable metal tape measure (leaving the 18" ruler in the drawer), we laid out the office to accept this major addition. Training was developed to assist Mt. Clemens staff members in mastering these new geographical areas. They would now be serving Roseville, Warren, St. Clair Shores, Centerline, and Van Dyke. Like all major personnel and customer records moves, it took planning and more planning. The execution went acceptably well. Loose ends dangled for a while.

Existing personnel in Roseville did receive a bit of orientation regarding the HO-ward exchange which was now a part of their responsibility. However, their task was relatively easy with only one new account name and rates to learn. In time, it all got integrated.

District Manager Birkhold was transferred to the Division Office to replace someone who was retiring. I think it may have been Jaxon Wysong.

Our new district manager was Bill Schweitzer. He had been a Sales Manager in a number of venues around the state. This was his first district manager assignment. We got along fine. After he had become acquainted with the happenings in the office, he called me down to his office. He asked if our recruiter was Athalee Dyer. I said she was indeed our recruiter. He said, "We do not have any minorities working in this office." I agreed. He gave me the responsibility of working with Mrs. Dyer and making the next two hires be minority women. Athalee and I had worked well together in the Trinity District, so we went shopping. First stop, a new department store just a bit out Gratiot from the office—Korvette. We discovered a minority lady selling hosiery in the women's department. Her name was Ann Cox. Athalee bought three pair of hose (at company expense of course). She invited Ann to visit our office the next day. Ann did. She tested very well. She toured the office. Athalee visited her home. Ann's husband was a management trainee with the Ford Motor Company, recently transferred from a California assembly plant. Ann was hired.

She became a valuable SR in the order unit. A very bright lady.

Athalee and I completed our assignment during a "shopping trip" to the Sears store on Gratiot Avenue across from the Valley-Walnut district office. There, a young minority woman was working in the women's dress department. I don't remember her name, but I do remember that she tested and interviewed very well. Her home visit was fine. Her husband had been a Detroit fireman for several years. She joined us in the Roseville office. The barrier was down, and brought with it two fine employees. Our new boss was pleased.

On Friday, May 8, 1964, a tornado struck Chesterfield Township, a portion of our Roseville District. The damage to homes and businesses was devastating. Thirteen people died and 400 were injured, and most of those hospitalized. A plan for such emergencies was always in place. The manger and three supervisors were on call for such occurrences.

Saturday, the four of us were in the building at Eleven-Mile and Gratiot in Roseville. We arrived at 8:00 a.m. A few calls arrived from customers and emergency agencies, e.g. police and fire departments. Our basic task was to write administrative orders for what was called in the practice and procedures binder "Reestab Fire."

Property damaged or destroyed would usually, over time, be repaired or rebuilt. Telephone service to that business or home would be put on hold, and held until a time when it could be reinstalled—"reestablished." Charges and services in the meantime were suspended. "Fire" included all such disabling events. Because this was not a common occurrence, we pulled the practices and procedures out of the bookcase and reviewed them, so that orders were properly prepared for the order typing crew on Monday morning.

The last piece of excitement involved the roof of the office. The cap on the porthole at the top of the ladder leading to the roof had blown partly off. Wind and rain were blowing into the passageway. Someone had to go up on the roof and secure the cap. I looked around, and without even a nomination, I was voted most eligible. It was approximately the same as being in a "hoochie" in Korea when it rained, but without the snipers.

I did not get to know Bill Schweitzer very well, as I was about to be transferred to the Walnut/Valley District order unit in Harper Woods.

One final hurrah before leaving the Roseville office was the annual installation of officers for our local Kiwanis group. For the occasion we had rented the private dining room on the second floor of Huck's Lakeshore Inn, at Nine-Mile Road and Jefferson. Members and their guests were given a variety of entrees to choose from. Wife Ginny and I selected duck under glass, with cherry sauce. The statewide president of Kiwanis was on hand to install local officers. He was Loren White. He and wife Celia ran a high-end interior decorator service named "The White House." Their business was located on Woodward Avenue in Ferndale. Dinner was superb. The wine was strong.

President Loren rose to perform the installations. These went off without a hitch. He then announced that he and Celia had a surprise for all the ladies present. Ceila would bestow on each Kiwanian wife the honorary title of "Kiwani Queen." At that moment I knew that my wife would never again attend another Kiwanis function. Luckily, two weeks later I was transferred to my new assignment in the Walnut/Valley order unit. We left Kiwanis behind.

‽

ORDER MANAGER—WALNUT/VALLEY: 1965

Being transferred to a second order manager's position in a city office was a bit of a downer. Walnut/Valley was considered a city office even though it was located in the town of Harper Woods. It was still south of Eight-Mile Road. In summary, I had now managed order units in both city and suburban settings, plus a billing unit in a large suburban area. I had heard some rumors that I was next in line for promotion to district manager. I had asked my Roseville boss Bill Schweitzer about this rumor. His response had been that this might not happen because of "equal opportunity" (EEOC), and the need for the corporation to promote minorities. This happened. Of course, I will never know if that district job was meant for me and taken by someone else due to EEOC considerations. The gentleman who received that next position in the commercial department was a friend of mine. He did not fare well over time, and was demoted twice. I lost track of him as he was transferred several times and eventually succumbed to alcoholism. Very sad.

My new district manager was John Cojeen. The billing manager was Fran Spowart. Tom Warth was the miscellaneous manager. The supervisory and SR staff was experienced and showed competency in all aspects of the job.

Business Office Supervisors Shirley Hunt and Ruth Ritscher are both remembered as keeping the office humming. Up until this time, office managers' desks were in the main part of the office, usually backed up against a wall. It was decided by the powers-that-be to provide managers with closed-in offices. These enclosures had waist-high metal walls with large windows for a broad view of the entire office. It was nice to have a tiny bit of privacy. This was accomplished over time with a great deal of expense. In my opinion we did not manage any better. Face-to-face personnel discussions still needed to be conducted in a private setting, e.g. a training or conference room. These little glass houses were too open for serious discussions, even with the door closed.

Sales were going well, as were accuracy, completeness, and timeliness measurements. Some tone deficiencies popped up occasionally, and some attitude adjusting was needed and administered. District Manager Cojeen favored an axiom from his former mentor, Commercial Department AVP Lou Conroy—*"To inspire others, be inspired."*

Mr. Cojeen was transferred to Saginaw, which happened to be his home town. Peter Grylls replaced John. Peter was a very experienced Business Office leader. He had begun his career as an SR in the Townsend District.

He had moved through the chairs on his way to this third-level district position. He believed in *"sincerely involving the team."* We were all willing to follow this tested leader. We did.

On July 23, 1967, Detroit exploded into a major race riot, which lasted for five days.

Managers in the commercial department were assigned to Traffic offices in Detroit to replace operators who did not show up for work. Driving over fire hoses, around police barricades, and hearing bullets whining overhead was not conducive to 100% attendance. Hence managers received marching orders based on where they lived, not where they worked. I lived in Royal Oak. My assignment was to report to the Northland parking lot in Southfield at 2:00 P.M.

on the Monday after the riot had begun on Sunday.

We boarded a Greyhound bus. Sitting in back of the driver was a National Guard member in full battle gear, cradling a Thompson sub-machine-gun. We were all impressed. This was serious. The bus wove its way through side streets from Southfield to the Trinity district office at 105 East Bethune, across from the Detroit mounted police division. I had worked in that building a few years back. There we picked up another contingent of managers and a Detroit policeman holding what he referred to as a riot gun (whatever that meant).

We descended into the "ditch" (actually the John Lodge freeway) heading south to the downtown Bell Building at 1365 Cass Avenue. We were to man operator switchboards on twelve-hour shifts. Out the right side (west) bus windows we could see fire and smoke. Out the left side windows (east) we could only see close up neighborhoods, but we could hear gun shots. They were flying over the bus. For me, it had been fourteen years since I had heard the whine of a bullet going overhead. That had been on Heartbreak Ridge in Korea.

Whoever was sitting next to me on the bus offered me a cigarette. I had been four years without one. I took it. When we arrived at the Bell Building, I took the elevator to the cafeteria and purchased a pack of Marlboros. When I got home from that first twelve-hour shift, Ginny joined me in having a cigarette after dinner. This sin lasted for circa two months after the riots ended. Then we quit for good.

◊

Here I will digress and explain about Bell Telephone employees at all levels of the organization. Managers peopling telephone switchboards happened not only during the Detroit riot scene, but also whenever there was a general strike by members of the Communications Workers of America. During my almost thirty-five years with the Company, I was called to strike duty only four times: two days in the Bell building located behind the Webster business office at Grand River and Oakman Boulevard, five days in the downtown Lansing Bell building, nine days in the downtown Pontiac Bell building, and finally fifteen days in the Upper Peninsula of Michigan at Iron Mountain. This last assignment began with being one of four managers selected to fly from City airport to Iron Mountain. There, we were picked up by a taxi and transported to the

Dickenson Inn hotel. This facility was located just the other side of the railroad tracks downtown. (No longer there.) The Bell building was two blocks away up a slight rise of ground. We checked in to our rooms, met for dinner at the locally famous T&T Steak House, and went to bed early, since we were on the 6:00 A.M. to 6:00 P.M. shift.

The railroad track ran close to the Inn. Trains were quite frequent as they were hauling Taconite (iron ore pellets) south to waiting blast furnaces. I left for my five-minute walk to the Bell Building at 5:30 A.M. As I crossed the tracks I picked up pieces of Taconite that had slipped off the open freight cars. I was a bit apprehensive about crossing the picket line. My previous experience of being bounced around a bit in Pontiac was on my mind. In Southfield at the accounting center, strikers were tossing spiked missiles under non-striker's autos to blow their tires. As I approached the Bell building entrance, two strikers with CWA signs came down the hill toward me. They were smiling, one man and one woman. They each extended a hand to shake.

I did. They asked, "are you from Detroit?" "Yes." "What time is your lunch hour?" I admitted honestly that I had no idea. They said "Whenever you go out for a meal, go to *'Ma Somebody's'* (I cannot remember). Some of us will be there and we would love to hear about what is happening in the big city areas, plus Ma has homemade wild huckleberry pie most days." I went.

It was all true. Friendly people galore. Telephone jobs, I found out, were coveted in that community. They were all in the Union to avoid trouble, but had no serious gripes about anything work related, even wages.

I received a new headset and a ten-minute familiarization session, and I was for the fourth time in my career operating a switchboard. There were many interesting, even memorable calls. The second call, however, was the winner.

I answered the signal "Operator," to hear a distraught lady say, "Oh good, please call the Sheriff, there is a bear in our tree, and I am afraid he will come down and kill my dog, who is barking up the tree. My dog will not come in the house and I am not going out to get him." I knew from the signal that she was calling from Bruce Crossing, so I got her address and alerted the Sheriff. The telephone business was forever fascinating, whether just routine or bear handling in the UP; it was all good. When we worked these twelve-hour shifts, six days on and then a mandatory one day off, we made an extraordinary amount of overtime money. I never quite understood it, but we were paid in quarter-hour increments. I took those big dollars and ran. No need to know how it was all computed.

Back in Detroit, I reported to my next assignment in the Billing Unit of the Woodward District.

☙

BILLING MANAGER— WOODWARD: 1967

The Woodward District was in the Gratiot Division. It was located in the Michigan Bell Headquarters building at 1365 Cass Avenue. The business office was in the northwest corner of the second floor. The overall layout was a bit smaller than the other three Commercial offices where I had worked. However, the work was much the same. My responsibility was the billing unit. There were two sections, supervised by two very experienced persons, Shirley Bloss and Mary Van Deventer. I don't recall the name of the training supervisor. She was also the relief supervisor.

I reported to the district manager, who was also very experienced. His name was Ralph C. Heid, but everyone called him Dutch. He was very well known. He lived in Plymouth with his wife and their nine children. He had the Michigan Bell "offspring" record, and his only competition was Tom McLaughlin, another commercial district manager. He and his wife had only eight children. Dutch managed on a theme: *"Love everybody— Change a little—Overlook a lot."* It had worked for him during his long career, and his managers paid attention. Bob Stunkel was the order manager for only a brief time after I arrived. He left suddenly. During the next three months, I had the opportunity to manage the order unit as well as billing. It was a short tenure. Hence, I have forgotten the names of the supervisors, except for Norma Gluba. Her experience, especially in writing small business orders, was extensive and memorable. In time a new order manager arrived in the person of Ruth Brown.

Everything was going smoothly in billing. Collections were being made at a solid pace. There was a large base of mostly business customers in the downtown area. They paid their bills promptly. Turnover of SR's was minimal. Experience was extensive. If you originally accepted a job in the heart of the city, you wanted to be there, and you did not leave because you wanted to be somewhere else.

Mr. Hcid offered me the opportunity to attend a management assessment program. This was a new offering by general personnel. The purpose was, to find second-level managers ready to fill district level positions in the future. At that time there were 329 district positions in the Company. This included all departments. I had been in the company for thirteen years, and a manager for eight years. My goal was a district level job. I agreed to give assessment a shot.

It was three days in length. It was intense. Two interviews by specially trained in-house district managers. Several written tests, including one focusing on knowledge of current events, city, state, national, and international. Exercises were split into two groups of six, until the last full day. For the final exercise the two groups came together. There was an unstructured task: a major undertaking to organize an imaginary company. Elect officers, select department heads, decide what kind of "widgets" to manufacture from the mass of "Tinker Toy" parts available from "suppliers" (the assessment staff). This exercise lasted all day, with the normal break for lunch. The observer assessors watched how each participant reacted and contributed, or didn't. Four assessors took copious notes in a prescribed format. An amazing, interesting, demanding adventure.

Two weeks later Dutch called me to his office to meet with the feedback assessor. I had scored acceptably, but not in the top-quartile. Summary: I was not aggressive enough, and he gave me examples of where I might change my behavior going forward in the real world. I didn't. However, it was for certain quite a learning experience.

Time ticked on in the Woodward billing unit. Dutch Heid received a call from George Fezzey. I had worked for George three times before. He had been asked to form a new group, the Mechanization Methods and Procedures district. Dutch and George met at Carl's Chophouse, on Grand River. Carl's was famous for buying blue ribbon beef from every possible fair statewide for his restaurant. Hundreds of blue ribbons lined the walls of this high-end establishment. It was here that these two district-level managers decided that it would be best if I moved from the line job to a staff position. George had an opening and arrangements were made for me to serve as a staff manager. I would be moving back to the Cass Adams building. That building, by the way, had been home to Ebling Creamery. The second floor was where the milk wagon horses had been housed. The ramp the horses used to ascend to that level was still intact in back of a large door at the rear of the building.

I reported to that office. George called me into his office and closed the door. He proceeded to tell me that he was leaving at the end of the month for a two- to three-year rotational assignment at AT&T in New York. He already had purchased a home in Murray Hill, New Jersey. My new leader would be Dave Beamer. WOW— Dave and his wife Nancy, a former SR, were great friends of ours from the First Presbyterian Church in Royal Oak. Small world. George left. Dave arrived. Thus began three years of interesting, demanding, and fruitful work with Dave Beamer and a sizeable team in the new Mechanization Methods District.

However, before this new position began, I was placed on a three-month special assignment with a General Personnel group named Management Assessment. This group had been formed to assess non-management employees for first-level supervisory assignments.

☙

MANAGEMENT ASSESSOR: 1968

Six managers from different departments were selected to be assessors. The universe of candidates to be assessed was selected from top-flight craft employees from several groups, e.g. installers, repairmen and women, operators, engineering assistants, service representatives, and others.

The assessment center was located on the first floor of the Statler hotel in downtown Detroit. This was a very plush set of suites used for interview rooms, testing sites, and group activities. I had been assessed here a few months earlier, for different purposes. However, some of the exercises were similar. The center was managed by Dave Hoyle, a comptroller's manager acting as district manager for the assessment project. His assistants were supervisors, both named Mary. They were very experienced. Two typists rounded out the team.

Eight people were assessed during a three-day event. Candidates were each interviewed, using a pre-set group of questions. Then they were given a battery of tests. The major assessment activity involved that long, involved group project to put together a company to manufacture widgets. I cannot remember what shapes were available, but there were many from which the group could choose. Some groups made many good decisions, got organized, bought parts from the suppliers (us assessors), and sold finished products in the market place to buyers (us assessors). Some kept books, issued P & L statements, and concocted an annual report.

Four of the six assessors were taking copious notes regarding the involvement of each candidate in the work group. The key to scoring well was to be involved as much as possible. To offer ideas and explain why they would work. To sell your ideas. To get things done without arousing resentment. When the three days ended for the participants, they were tired, and happy to be done with this trying experience. For us assessors, the work had just begun. Having been in session all day, Monday through Wednesday, we each now had two days to collect and summarize all information on two of the participants. The two assessors who were not observers at the last group exercise would still be full participants in the final evaluations. Duties rotated each week for each assessor.

After lunch each Friday we assembled around a long oval boardroom table and began the process of assessing each of the eight candidates who had been in the assessment process that week. Each candidate was presented via test scores and interviews, and we reviewed the results of each activity, including details of contributions made by each candidate during the long demanding widget-building exercise.

Assessors had been trained to do this job to perfection. Leader Hoyle and his assistants had taken us through this process several times, with "live" materials from prior assessments. We were ready. We were serious. We wanted to get it right. We did. After much review and discussion each of the eight candidates was placed in what we agreed was their proper quartile. It was seldom that this Friday afternoon meeting ended before 7:00 P.M. Sometimes way beyond. No one complained. No one expected to be paid extra. It was a compelling assignment that we all coveted. We became a team. Remembering some of the assessors: Floyd Allen, Duke Helmrich, Addison Johnson, Joe Lang, Marge (surname lost), along with others.

One final step was providing feedback to the candidate, his or her immediate boss, and his or her district manager. After two weekly sessions, we distributed the sixteen feedbacks, each of us taking responsibility for two or three depending on where the employee was located. Appointments were made, and that is what we did that week. That short week in part accounted for there being no complaints for those late Fridays.

During my time at the Statler, I found out that the hotel concierge could and would obtain tickets for sporting events. She obtained the tickets and tacked on a charge of $1.25 per ticket. Denny McLain, a Detroit Tiger pitcher, was pitching on a Saturday trying for his record-setting thirtieth victory. The concierge obtained four tickets for me. My wife and two sons attended the game. It was a thriller, as the Tigers rallied in the ninth inning to win it for Denny's thirtieth victory. One other "thrill" for Ginny was that David Eisenhower and Julie Nixon were sitting three rows in front of us. Ginny even watched the game—occasionally.

When the end of my time as an assessor arrived, I was offered a feedback assignment in the Upper Peninsula from the two previous sessions.

I leapt at the opportunity. With travel and feedback appointments, it would consume a week. So, I set up appointments with each district manager: Plant two, Commercial one, and Traffic one. They in turn agreed to get the candidate and his or her boss on the same schedule. These district offices were in the Upper Peninsula, in Marquette, Michigan.

My wife Ginny and I packed our 1966 tan Ford station wagon, our two sons, ages eight and ten, an ironing board to press my suit each evening, and enough gear to stay a "month." We traveled on Monday, and I conducted one feedback on Tuesday, two on Wednesday, one on Thursday, and travelled home on Friday. The balance of each day was spent having a great vacation. This included searching the Lake Superior beach for Petoskey stones.

In Marquette we stayed in a one-of-a-kind motel, named the Tiroler Hof. It sat on the top of a high hill on the outskirts of the city. It had been built by a couple who had moved there from Austria and received a federal Small Business loan. It had an Alpine motif, which included a short ski run, and a tiny chapel copied from their home church in Europe. There was a full-service dining room serving breakfast and dinner, with two different entrees each evening. We thrived. The lads thought they were in the Alps.

The feedbacks went well. Two candidates scored in the top quartile, one mid-range, one in the lower quartile. Those are the tough ones to give feedback on. As it turned out this fourth candidate was the first of the four promoted to a supervisory position. "One never knows, does one?"

Back home, working on my expense account, I realized that this would turn out to be a very inexpensive family vacation. Total mileage was 1,100 at $.09 per mile (1968), bridge toll $7.00 each way, motel expense two standard beds priced the same no matter the number of occupants (queens and kings unheard of), my meal expense zero, family meal expense nominal. Thus the total cost of a weeklong family vacation in the Upper Peninsula of Michigan was all but nil.

On Monday I reported to Dave Beamer, district manager in Mechanization Methods, in the Cass Adams building. I found a desk, a chair, a file cabinet, and where to get a cup of coffee. Supplied the desk with basics. Read a few update memos from the new group. Dave Beamer arrived. He was to lead a fairly large team in this new district— Mechanization Methods. Our first order of business was to arrange our move into new quarters in Southfield.

During the short time before we moved from the Cass Adams building, I had arranged to become a candidate to teach the Dale Carnegie Course.

This would be moonlighting. If I completed the training and became a certified instructor, I would be teaching on average one four-hour session, one evening per week, for twenty-eight weeks per year. I asked my new leader, Mr. Beamer, to arrange a meeting with his boss, division manager Whit Jones, so I could ask for approval to become an instructor. He did this, and at the same time wanted me to present the details of how we planned to handle White Pages Directory listings using the new order-typing system. I put this information together, to present to "The Whitter" which is what we called Mr. Jones, but not to his face. I created an example of how these listings would be laid out. Feeling clever as I proceeded, I said "for example, take a 'common' name like Jones." Mr. Jones arose from his chair saying "Jones is a frequently used name, but it is for certain not common." Whoops, not so clever, and then I had to ask for approval to moonlight teaching the Dale Carnegie course. Not to worry. I asked. Whit said that that is entirely up to your boss. Dave Beamer and I attended the same church. My wife sang in the choir with him, his wife Nancy, and his brother Jim. I now had my new leader's official permission to teach.

☙

INSTRUCTOR—DALE CARNEGIE & ASSOCIATES: 1968—1976
(MOONLIGHTING)

Preparations to become a Dale Carnegie instructor were very challenging. The many steps began with taking the course—fourteen consecutive weeks of instruction from 6:00 P.M. to 10:00 P.M. The cost in 1957 was $250.00. Remember, my boss Frank Philips had suggested that I needed this training. I had borrowed the money from the Telephone Employees Credit Union and enrolled.

Class size was set at forty-four, a maximum because of class time constraints. At the end of each fourteen-week session, the instructor, graduate assistants, the secretary, and the class voted to select those class members they thought would make effective graduate assistants. The vote was via secret ballot and results were not revealed to the class. They knew this before they voted. The purpose of this exercise was to select potential candidates to be offered an opportunity to become graduate assistants for future classes.

The top four vote-getters were then given that opportunity.

I was very fortunate to be one of the four selected when I took the course. Thus, I became a graduate assistant (GA) for two full sessions, twenty-eight weeks. We set up chairs and tables, answered questions, and dealt with whatever needed attention. Our most important function was to give sample talks in front of the group, to help class members better prepare their talks. Sample talks were always given before the class ended to demonstrate talks class members would be preparing for next week's session. Each class had a paid secretary to do clerical chores, take tuition payments, hand out books and pamphlets, enroll walk-ins, and whatever other business needs surfaced. Instructors had a solid support team. Class members had to be served.

Graduate Assistants became the source for future instructor candidates. Anyone selected to become an instructor candidate was interviewed by the owner of the local Dale Carnegie Licensing Agreement. Being invited to participate in instructor training was not a guarantee of certification as an instructor. The success rate was less than 50%. I received an offer to become an instructor candidate. I accepted. This was after having participated as a graduate assistant in forty-two four-hour class meetings, three full classes of fourteen weeks each. I was about to try for certification as a Dale Carnegie instructor, to be one of only 1,700 in the world.

Training consisted of fourteen days in a row (two full weeks), from 3:00 P.M. to 12:00 midnight. The first three hours were to prepare for the four-hour session to follow, with a live class. This class was sold at one-half regular price, because of the trainee status of instructors. The quality of the learning did not suffer, because the chief instructor was Paul Mackey Ph.D., second-in-command of Dale Carnegie worldwide. He was headquartered in Garden City, N.Y. Mrs. Dorothy Carnegie was the owner.

Amazing, but I did it. Do not ask how. My Michigan Bell office was located in Southfield, at Number One Northland Drive. Those fourteen-days-in-a-row sessions were to be located in Stouffer's Inn, not far from the office. My boss, Dave Beamer, allowed me to take one week of vacation in half-days, and even allowed me to get to work a tad early. I arrived at 7:30 A.M. Then I left for home at 11:30 A.M. Arrived home at 12:00 noon. Wife Ginny had a dinner meal ready. Ate slowly. Took a forty-five-minute nap. Showered, dressed, and was back on the road by 2:15 P.M. to arrive at the Inn's training suite by 2:45 P.M. for the 3:00 P.M. start time.

Each evening after the class members had departed, Dr. Mackey held forth in a two-hour (10:00 P.M.—midnight) training session to review the previous four hours. It is impossible to explain the dynamics, except to say that the learning was intense. One tiny example: we sat in comfortable chairs in a circle. He would select a candidate and say to him e.g. "Russ tell Bob everything you saw him do or say this evening in front of the group that you thought was done well." Everyone received an opportunity to be on both the giving and receiving end of that positive critique, remembering back to those previous four hours. The dynamics of those moments, even though it was nearly midnight, were unbelievable to me. Carnegie training focuses only on the positive.

At the completion of these fourteen days, Dr. Mackey delivered a one-on-one complete evaluation of each candidate's performance. Those who did not make the grade to become certified instructors were told in miniscule detail why. Those who qualified as future instructors were also told in miniscule detail why they were certified.

The final step before being given a Dale Carnegie class of your own, with two GA's, a secretary, and a room full of class members, was that you had to co-teach twice with a certified (experienced) instructor. During those twenty-eight sessions the new instructor was paid one-half of an instructor's remuneration. It was well known that the senior instructor did nothing but show up and sit. That was to give the new man (all men in those days) lots of real-life experience in front of those groups.

I was required to co-teach for two sessions—twenty-eight weeks. I was now earning money: $32.50 per four-hour session. My mentor instructor did in fact do nothing. He earned $65.00 per session. I learned a lot. I was ready to go it alone. So, after a year of getting ready, I was given my first full-blown class. Now I was realizing $65.00 per session, $910.00 per fourteen weeks of instruction.

It would not be fair to try to explain the dynamics of the Dale Carnegie course on paper. It needs to be experienced. The complexities of learning a variety of human relations skills, plus developing skills necessary to speak effectively in front of a group, or one on one, are infinite. When speaking in public it is recognized that we all have butterflies. The course gets them flying in formation. We need them to be there to energize our presentation, but we also need them to be under control. The axioms, suggestions, and rules introduced in these fourteen four-hour learning sessions are presented in such unique ways that they stay with class members for as long as they live. Dale Carnegie instructors love what they do, and it shows.

I taught for seven years—196 four-hour sessions, or 784 hours of classroom time—helping 616 different class members. I would have done it for free, as I had done as a Graduate Assistant. However, those moonlight dollars were always welcome. I taught at a variety of Michigan venues: Royal Oak, Troy, Jackson, Warren, South Lyon, and Southfield. I had an opportunity to teach on the island of Jamaica, on a two-week package deal. Unfortunately, I was unable to make that fit in with my day job at the phone factory.

On occasion a Dale Carnegie course graduate will be maligned by a person saying something like "Don't treat me with any of that Carnegie stuff." The return question then is "How would you like me to treat you"?

That return question is supported by a multitude of ways in which the course opens us up for honest, sincere, candid, direct communications with our fellow human beings. This makes for success in every part of life, including friendships.

I retired from my position as a certified Dale Carnegie instructor at the end of 1976. I was forty-eight years old. Teaching this dynamic course is both physically and emotionally demanding. I decided to "hang 'em up" before I began not to be satisfied with my presentations. It had been a great run. After seven productive years, the time was right. Younger men and now women were at the ready to take over. Women were at last entering the instructor's role, where in the past they were only involved as instructors in the Dorothy Carnegie course designed for and taught exclusively by women.

I stepped immediately into a new moonlighting job, as an adjunct instructor at Wayne State University, teaching in the after-hours management development program for General Motors employees at the Tech Center in Warren, Michigan.

☙

INSTRUCTOR—WAYNE STATE UNIVERSITY: 1976—1979
(MOONLIGHTING)

My friend Mac McVicar had taught a course for Wayne State University at the General Motors Technical Center in Warren, Michigan, for many years.

He lived miles away from the training site and finally decided to give up this moonlighting position, to teach closer to home. He suggested that I might want to take over this position.

He was presenting a technical course that I was not qualified to teach, so it meant my obtaining approval to change to a management curriculum that I would be qualified to deliver. Mac reported to a Miss Nancy Hernandez. She in turn reported to Roy E. Robinson. This gentleman had been the principal of my grade school forty-four years earlier. All my early report cards contain his stamped signature. He had then moved to the Ferndale, Michigan, school district as superintendent of schools. After he retired he accepted an administrative post at Wayne State

University in Detroit. We met and reminisced. Approval was granted.

General Motors personnel management agreed to the change. I designed a supervisor/manager/leadership curriculum, centering on "Involving the team in a meaningful way." Each session was two hours long, from 6:30 P.M. to 8:30 P.M. for eight consecutive weeks. This was one of several continuing education courses offered by Wayne State to G.M. employees. All classrooms were located in the Chevrolet engineering building in Warren, Michigan. I taught three or four of these eight week courses each year for three years. The stipend was $75.00 per night for two hours. During those years I occasionally enhanced the course with new material, staying with the same theme.

For me, it was very interesting work, and only three miles from home.

○ʒ

STAFF MANAGER—
MECHANIZATION METHODS:
1969

This newly formed district was located at 1922 Cass Avenue in the central part of the city of Detroit. There was very little on-street parking, and it was not an area where one could safely leave an auto. Just under two blocks from the building was Fred's parking lot. It included his "all by hand" auto wash. He preferred arranging a weekly parking rate, which in essence gave you one-half day free. Fred was the epitome of a really fine fellow. The lot was guarded from 6:00 A.M. until 6:00 P.M. Parkers were advised not to leave anything of value in the auto, even though it would be locked and watched. If you planned to be later than 6:00 P.M., special arrangements could be made with Fred. I knew that we would soon be moving, so I signed up for one month and paid the fee, to include a weekly auto wash. This was my second tour with Fred.

Thus began my second assignment in the Cass Adams building, where the Ebling Creamery horses had preceded me. The first trip had been with Commercial Methods. This new assignment was in Mechanization Methods. District Manager Dave Beamer assembled a team of four Managers, eight first-level supervisors, and one district secretary. We met that first day to receive our assignments. Simple. To move all of us into new quarters at "Number One Northland Drive," Southfield, Michigan. We did it in short order.

However, in the month before we moved we experienced a bit of comic relief, although in some ways a serious matter. In the Cass Adams Building district managers and above had their name and floor number listed in white plastic letters in a glassed-front locked case. The first-floor lobby did not have a security person on duty, as many buildings had begun to have. This area of town harbored some men and women wandering about, many carrying a bottle in a brown paper bag, usually with the top off.

Listings on the lobby wall directory contained two initials, plus the person's last name and floor number. So, our boss was listed as D.R. Beamer— Third Floor. On four occasions in the first week we were in the building, some local folks took the elevator to the third floor looking for "Doctor Beamer." When told Mr. Beamer was not a doctor, those were only his initials, some of the visitors spied the bathroom and availed themselves of that service. When the fourth visitor had departed without seeing the doctor, Dave's secretary, Addie Gillespie, gave him the details. Dave called the building manager and asked her to change D.R. to "Dave." She agreed to do that immediately, and did. He then called Jack Penland. Jack had had a long career with the Detroit police department, and was now leading Michigan Bell corporate security. Dave told him the story, and recommended that 1922 Cass be designated as a lobby needing a uniformed receptionist. Happily for the occupants of the Cass Adams building, that happened one month after we had moved to Southfield.

Mrs. Pak Sundeen was the commercial department furniture and equipment administrator. She advised us that there was not sufficient furniture in storage to serve our new district, hence we would need to purchase all new items. She put us in contact with Joe Schutz. He was a manufacturer's representative for a variety of companies. He brought catalogs. We selected black metal desks with walnut grained Formica tops. The order was for fourteen double-pedestal desks with matching black fabric-covered chairs, fourteen two-drawer lockable file cabinets, two large office files, waste baskets for all, and other office paraphernalia. Big order, even for Joe. Hence, he promised "within-thirty-days" delivery. He kept his promise. We moved.

The goal of this new operation was to research, design, develop, and implement a system to transmit service orders from a business office to the plant department assignment office, by typing the orders on a cathode ray tube and hitting a key to activate the teletype machines in the installation department.

This avoided several steps in the order writing and transfer process.

The learning curve for District Manager Beamer and his four managers began with a visit to the cathode ray tube manufacturer, the Sanders Corporation, in Nashua, New Hampshire. Up until this time Sanders had mostly been involved in producing electronic equipment for the U.S. Navy. We flew there on the Sanders corporate jet. It was a windy November night. We landed in the middle of an ice storm. According to the pilots, there was less than two feet left of the tarmac when the plane finally slid to a stop. This assignment was starting out to be very exciting, maybe even dangerous.

Dave was definitely the boss. He was super smart, and a fast learner. He gave each of us explicit instructions and a timetable, and left us to do it. We did. The test district was Southfield, very close to our office. The plant district where the orders were to end up was also nearby.

During the three years this team worked for Mr. Beamer, he and three of his managers played golf every nice Friday morning at the Rackham golf club. This was a public course on the north side of Ten-Mile Road just west of Woodward Avenue. It was never clear to me what municipality owned this course. It was very well-maintained, well-known because Joe Louis often played there with a contingency of his friends. Our tee time was 6:30 A.M. We played nine holes. Back home circa 9:00 A.M. After a shower, shave, shine, and shampoo we all reached the office by 11:00 A.M. After a check of the mail, plus an update from our staffs, we grabbed a sandwich at the little Greek restaurant down the hall. About 12:30 P.M. (remember this was always on Friday) our group met in Dave's office to begin contract bridge lessons. He taught both beginners and experienced players at the same time, as we played real hands. The one non-golfer joined us. This went on along with lunch. We folded the bridge game at 2:30 P.M. and finished off the day doing our various tasks. The four managers desks were lined up under the windows at the rear of the large office. Two supervisor's desks were located in front of each manager. The staff had been handpicked: Lee Wallace, Rita Chester, Norma Gluba, Jane Duffy, Phillis Cook, Connie Martin, John Cribb, Bill Harvey, Lon Kain, and me.

So, you are saying, WOW—not bad —golf and bridge every Friday, mostly on company time. Were these freeloaders earning their salaries? The answer is a definitive yes, and more. The only time we could shut down the Southfield business office systems to work on them was on the weekend. Over a fifteen-month period we worked eight hours on Saturday and four hours on Sunday, three weekends out of each month. This was because we spent Saturday morning taking down the working system.

Afternoons were used to install and test the trial system. Sunday morning was spent taking down that system and re-installing the regular system. This was then tested several times to be certain all was well. If the orders did not flow easily through the regular channel on Monday mornings, we would have been in more trouble than your imagination could possibly dream up. This work time was all gratis, with no overtime remuneration, except of course contract bridge lessons, and nine holes of golf. We loved it: the challenge, accomplishments, visiting firemen from other Bell operating companies looking over our shoulders, often in awe, plus plaudits from AT&T.

Remember this began in 1969. Prior to this, orders for telephone service has been written by hand, then typed on a teletype machine in an order-typing room. Now orders would be typed on a cathode ray tube 'screen' and sent via teletype directly from the order taker (SR) to the assignment group in the installation department. This may not sound like a big deal, but there have been fifty-one years of order processing developments since then.

The Mechanization Methods district continued to operate at full speed. The order processing experiment closed. Cathode ray tubes became far more sophisticated. New projects arrived almost daily. I requested a transfer to the Management Training and Education District in the Personal Department (later named Human Resources). Mr. Beamer agreed to check out that possibility. He did. Luck struck. Hoyce Wrather, district manager of that training district was looking for a second-level manager as a staff-instructor to replace Jerry Wendel, who was transferring to a newly formed internal consulting group led by district manager Carl Hill.

Mr. Wrather lived in Birmingham, Michigan, hence our "Number One Northland Drive" address was on his way home. He set up an appointment with me for a Friday afternoon at 2:00 P.M. Mr. Beamer suggested that he would leave early, so we could use his office for our meeting. The short story is that Hoyce and I clicked. We talked over the issues involved in delivering courses on relatively complex subjects in front of the group. Hoyce was most happy to find a manager who was already a trained instructor, from teaching the Dale Carnegie course. He said that I would be replacing a very talented Jerry Wendel. I probably should have been scared, but I wasn't. I was transferred. Thus began fifteen years of happiness doing—and later leading—the work that I had admired when I was a conferee in that first-level supervisory training course (IBMC) at the Fort Shelby Hotel, back in 1954—eighteen years earlier.

છ

INSTRUCTOR—MANAGEMENT TRAINING: 1972

Dreams do come true. I was now at work in the Personnel department in the Management Training and Education district. Hoyce Wrather was my new leader. My first assignment was to observe the five-day Interdepartmental Basic Management Course (IBMC). This course for newly appointed first-level supervisors had been in existence for many years. I had taken this training seventeen years earlier (1955). It had been updated several times.

The instructors I was observing were Carolyn Field and Jerry Wendel. The first thing I noticed was how well they worked together. When one of them was in front of the group, the other one was sitting unnoticed at the back of the room. When the presenter missed a point, or additional instruction was appropriate, from the back of the room would come an offhand comment, like "one other thing which is sometimes appropriate is...." What followed was an important point that had been missed by the upfront team member.

However, class members would not be aware of the omission, as the team smoothed it all out.

I watched and listened, all but hidden in back of a large easel. I took copious notes. I imagined myself in front of those twelve conferees, guiding them through five days of a basic leadership development agenda. I could hardly wait. I was not the only one behind an easel. Across from me behind another easel was Julie Heidt. She was also prepping to teach this course. We compared notes, and guessed that the next IBMC session, two weeks hence, would be ours to co-train. We agreed that we would be bailing each other out as Carolyn and Jerry had done.

Management training is costly. Twelve conferees off their job for five days. Two instructors in place. Training materials. Conferees living in the hotel where the training facilities were located. Lunch served in the hotel dining room or a conference room. So why provide this introduction to management? In the case of Michigan Bell Telephone Company, it was seen as the best way to introduce newly-appointed supervisors to their unfamiliar role as leaders. It also supported the unwritten policy of "promoting from within."

Each course segment was aimed at doing just that. The method was, for the most part, a seminar. Participation was the manner in which every topic was explored by the group, sometimes all twelve participants, but more often split into groups of six and with reports out of each group to the reassembled group of twelve.

Lecture contents included the place of Michigan Bell within the Bell System. Michigan Bell was in those days 4.6% of the entire Bell System. This included twenty-two operating companies besides Michigan; Western Electric, the supply arm for all companies, furnishing pencils, switch boards, MCF (million conductor feet) of cable, toilet paper, and beyond; Bell Labs; AT&T Long Lines (carrying calls out of the state and out of the country); plus Sandia Corporation, a wholly-owned subsidiary of AT&T working mostly with the U.S. Government on special communications needs. Studying all of this with new supervisors was meant to instill the feeling that even though the Company was massive, it all boiled down to individual segments that each of us was responsible to supervise.

One segment in IBMC explored the extinction of an age-old management style nicknamed KITA (Kick in The Ass). During these seminars there were almost always a few horror stories about real life experiences of being on the receiving end of this supervisory style. In the end, the instructional objective was to move solidly toward axioms like "*Supervising is teaching.*" Plus, there was an acceptance that a contemporary style was to "*Be Firm—Friendly—Fair,*" which was much touted as superior to KITA.

There was a segment on teamwork: within groups, between departments, and, in some instances, between companies. Out of these discussions came an understanding that strong leaders usually "*sincerely involve the team*" in a variety of ways.

On Thursday afternoon a problem-solving model was introduced. Just as the work day ended, each conferee was asked to do the only homework of the week: write down a problem that they knew about from their current or past work place. This would be used the next day to practice applying a problem-solving model. This entire segment was supported by the adage: "*A problem well-defined, is a problem one-half solved.*"

So, for one week these newly appointed first-level supervisors began to see the difference between doing the job themselves and guiding others in doing it. This is a big step. In many instances the new supervisor was now the boss in the same group where she or he had been a worker. When possible, these conferees were placed in the same training group of six so that this particular situation could be addressed. Discussion usually got around to talking about how the best worker would not necessarily make the best leader. With minor exceptions all of these conferees had been through the assessment center, and had scored well.

IBMC had received high marks forever. Even those employees who had been eager to become part of the management team had a few anxious moments when it finally happened. For the most part, this week of talking about, hearing about, and participating in a variety of planned exercises aimed at making them comfortable in taking charge of a group did the job it was intended to do. Everyone felt more prepared. Plus, almost all agreed that the Company was recognizing them with some top-flight training, at considerable cost. High praise indeed.

The next step as an instructor in the Management Training and Education District was to deliver the basic course for existing second-level Managers, titled Advanced Management Skills (AMS).

This six-day package was designed, developed, and implemented by Verne Jones, on loan from the Plant department. He was working on a Masters degree in organizational development at Pepperdine University in California. The course logistics included a four-day package of activities, with a two-day follow-up session circa three weeks later. This did not work out. Our registrar quickly found rescheduling of busy managers for a return engagement to be impossible. Several minor revisions rearranged the course into a five-day continuous package.

Instruction was aimed at recognizing the strength of the group, be it within your department, between departments, and between companies.

There were several segments to support this premise, including a set of axioms like *"Recognize the good work of others"* and *"Confident managers accept those who are different."*

One major activity was purchased from a management training vendor. It was a survival exercise. The group (our managers) had been on a routine flight and had run out of fuel, forced to land in the desert or the arctic. Twenty items were rescued from the plane before it burned. The task of the group was to assign a number to each item based on deciding what was most valuable for survival (#1) to what was least valuable (#20). The one hour and fifteen minutes allotted to this exercise was videotaped by one instructor while the second instructor was observing and taking notes.

When the predetermined time was up, we all went to a planned lunch.

Discussion continued. Upon our return the video was replayed, stopped on occasion, rewound, and replayed to demonstrate a learning point. Amazing how the group discovered their own strengths and deficiencies. Reaction to this learning exercise was exciting. The learning was automatic. Occasionally the instructor who had been taking notes would make a point which needed airing, but mostly the lessons were self-taught. It was very different working with a group of second-level peers than with first-level supervisors. Big challenge. Big fun. The five days always moved by quickly.

AT&T had purchased the rights from an international management training and development vendor to teach a problem-solving course to second- and third-level managers. This vendor is still doing business today, with a variety of different products. This was a three-day course. It contained several analytical tools not unlike those a consultant would use in determining the cause(s) of deficiencies in a particular work group, or with a process.

I spent a week in a New York hotel learning the training material. This was a very interesting week. I remember it well, not only for the course content, but because I had my left foot elevated on a chair the entire week. A Saturday morning tennis mishap had torn up my calf, causing my foot to become very dark. Upon return to Michigan, my task was to deliver this training material to the instructional staff, including our leader Mr. Wrather. It all went smashingly well, and the course gave those who partook—and there were many—a profound look at how performance deficiencies might be analyzed and corrected.

Another special training session was developed in 1974 after the filing of the U.S. Department of Justice's anti-trust lawsuit against AT&T. It was then that the Antitrust Division of the Federal Government had begun to consider whether or not the Bell System was "really" a "natural monopoly." Telephone companies had operated under that protective umbrella from their conception. AT&T developed this course to alert management employees to the dangers of acting like a monopoly, and especially to warn them not to keep certain documentation in files which might prove the case for dissolution of the Bell System. Michigan Bell began the process of presenting this one-day session (course). Instructors from the training district were assigned to teach with a company attorney. Sessions were scheduled in every division: Fort, Gratiot, Woodward, Southern (Grand Rapids), Northern (Saginaw), and the General Staff. In each case, local managers were trained to carry the antitrust message to all management personal in their area. The course material was exemplary. It contained a video which became a classic. It was a very compelling message.

ೞ

Note: In January 1982 the Bell System would be taken apart (divested) by Judge Green. It has been debated as to whether this was a positive or a negative step for the communications industry as a whole. Most likely it had to be done, to unleash the huge potential of cellular. Charlie Brown (seriously) was the president of AT&T at the time. He consented to the consent degree, dissolving the Bell System as we knew it.

ೞ

CORPORATE PERFORMANCE CONSULTANT: 1975

By 1975, I had spent three years as a management training instructor. I had had the opportunity to redesign several segments of basic courses. I co-trained and individually taught many sessions. I learned a lot during every session.

Division manager Bill Bowerman in the Directory department White Pages asked Jack Knaff, the division manager to whom my boss reported, if his training staff would be able to do a consultant-type analysis of the White Pages compilation group. Deficiencies were occurring and apparently these were caused by the system, not necessarily the staffing. It was decided somewhere up in the executive suite that I would be the person to utilize our newly-introduced problem-solving techniques, recommended by AT&T and now taught to a bevy of Michigan Bell managers. It was further decided that I would be promoted from "L" level manager to "G" level. This was considered a third-level position, with the benefits of a standard salary increase plus invitations to corporate meetings called for third-level-and-above managers. Many referred to this specialized title as a "2.5-level position rounded off."

The goal in Directory was to complete research, analysis, and prepare recommendations within forty-five days. I did it. It meant long days doing inspections, conducting interviews three days per week for several weeks, and doing summaries on weekends and late nights. This was a fascinating endeavor. Directory department management at all levels was very cooperative. Craft personnel were the same. The method we had taught to many managers really worked. The final report was used by the directory department managers as a flowchart to track inaccuracies and omissions in the White Pages. In time, systems were changed. During that period of time the training package consulting system was used to good effect. I returned to the role of instructor in the management training district. It was good to be back on a more normal schedule.

The reason I had been working as an internal performance consultant is because I was *not* in New York working for AT&T. In 1975, three years after I had left the Mechanization Methods district for the management training district, I received an offer for a two-year to three-year rotational assignment at AT&T. This would have meant an immediate promotion from manager to district manager. I had been waiting for that event to occur for quite some time.

The reason for this promotional opportunity was because I had been in on the ground floor when order processing codes were being developed for use in transmitting orders via Sanders cathode ray tube screens. Universal Service Order Codes (USOC's) were now to be installed in all twenty-three Bell operating companies coast to coast. A district manager was needed to spearhead the effort, plus supervise three managers who would introduce these codes and corresponding methods nationwide. It was estimated that this onetime project would require just under three years.

Decision time had arrived for Ginny and me once again. At last, an opportunity to become a district manager! I began to lay out a decision matrix *à la* Mark Twain—Pros and Cons. The laying out did not get very far. I decided to not accept the AT&T offer. The "cons" built up too fast to even begin the "pros". Most importantly, I enjoyed the work I was doing as a management training instructor. I was certain I would not enjoy riding herd on USOC codes across the US of

A. "Cons" continued to build: two sons at the University of Michigan would be paying massive out-of-state tuition (unless we gamed the system and changed their home address to their grandparents). We were comfortable with our Royal Oak Church, our sixteen-member potluck group, my three tennis partners; we had aging parents all living in Michigan, and sons with ongoing jobs in summers and over holidays at the Sign-of-the-Beefeater restaurant (later renamed Beef Carver).

Amazingly, once I had formally rejected the AT&T offer, along came that opportunity for a promotion part way to district level, while continuing to work in the management training district in Michigan.

I had been in the Management training and Education district as an instructor, then as a Performance Consultant, for five years. In June 1977, I was assigned to a special project reporting to Ken McLarty, a division manager (an IMDP who was moving very fast up the ladder of success). My assignment was to assist him in designing, developing, and delivering a President's Conference, the first such affair in eighteen years. This was a very meaningful, exciting, fulfilling assignment. I had been a

Michigan Bell management employee for twenty-three years.

☙

CO-DIRECTOR—MBT PRESIDENT'S CONFERENCE: 1977

On the first Monday in June, 1977, I was transferred from the Management Training and Education district reporting to Hoyce Wrather, to the very new "Management Consulting District" reporting to district manager Carl Hill. His other managers were Verne Jones and Jerry Wendall. This new assignment lasted for only two days. Mr. Hill was asked to send me for an interview with Division Manager Ken McLarty. It was a long interview.

Ken was an IMDP on an even faster track than your garden-variety IMDP.

He had been hired at Virginia Beach, Virginia, as he was being discharged from the Navy. His four-year tour of duty had ended. Cannot remember his rank, but I think Commander. Corporate recruiters had swarmed over these young discharged Naval officers. Ken had offers from IBM and AT&T. He selected the latter, and ended up with Michigan Bell. Full steam ahead he had just completed his fifth year at Michigan Bell. He was already Division level. He had a new assignment, and needed a third-level assistant.

Michigan Bell President David K. Easlick had asked his executive vice president (second in command) David Wenger to arrange for a week-long interdepartmental conference to include all third-level-and-above management personnel. He hoped this could begin in the fall (1977) and end in early 1978. Dave had two primary objectives: 1. Review the recently completed corporate five-year plan; 2. Reinforce corporate commitment to keep service to customers as our primary goal. Methods and procedures as to how to accomplish this were to be left to those who would be designing and developing the conference. The last President's conference had been in 1959— eighteen years earlier.

Dave Easlick was an interesting study in leadership. I had been informally introduced to him in 1956. I was reporting to Bob Tripp in the commercial methods group. He had known Dave since they were co-workers in Flint, Michigan, when Dave was a college trainee. Bob had come up through the ranks. Back then they were both second-level managers. This particular day Bob and I were returning from lunch. We stepped into an elevator in the headquarters building. Dave Easlick was already in the elevator.

He had just been promoted to Personnel Vice President. This was on his return from a full school year at Williams College, a very small, prestigious liberal arts institution in Massachusetts. He had participated in a specially designed learning experience for corporate executives. It was laughingly—yet accurately—referred to as "finishing school." Dave Easlick had been written about and pictured in "Ladies Home Journal" magazine, standing in his dorm room with a stack of books piled shoulder high. He and his classmates at Williams were purportedly going to read all of these tomes during the school year. More importantly they would be exposed to the elite life of New York city, i.e. opera, symphony, all manner of art and history museums, ballet, book reviews, fine dining, et.al. This was because, in their home communities, corporate officers were forever being asked to attend programs for the arts, serve on boards, raise funds for all sorts of institutions and endeavors. Most of these men (all men in those days) had business educations. Fine arts had been either totally ignored or at best neglected.

But I digress. My boss and I had just stepped into the elevator. Bob greets Dave, introduces me. We shake hands. Bob says "Wow Dave, what a great thing for you to be back in your home company as VP of Personnel." The new VP says twice for emphasis; "Bob, it's the money! It's the money!" Dave in time became the president of Michigan Bell. He took his work very seriously. He did not seem to take himself seriously, which made him fun to be around, and gave him our respect and loyalty.

Back to my interview with Ken McLarty. The interview ended well for me, with a job offer to join him in designing, developing, and delivering this major conference. We shook hands. We agreed to begin the process the next morning in his office. He said that the first order of business was to develop a PERT Chart. I remembered reading about that technique in National Geographic magazine. It had been developed by the U. S. Navy in the 1950s to manage the Polaris submarine missile program. PERT decoded "Program Evaluation Review Technique." Commander McLarty was very much at home with this Navy-developed system, and very willing to teach it to his "new internal hire"—me.

It is impossible to completely detail our process. We spent two days listing every possible activity and item needed to complete preparations for this major conference, plus setting a start and completion date for each item. Our list exceeded 1,000 entries. Three more days were spent committing these activities to large sheets of specially bleached heavy white Kraft paper. These were taped to the office walls in two tiers, the top tier slightly above eye level. Every item needing to be accomplished was placed in sequence, thus insuring that each item would be done on time to allow the next one to follow. This was the valuable part of PERT charting.

We wrapped up the week's work of ten-hour days. I had reported to Ken McLarty for five business days. He sat behind his desk. I sat in the visitor's chair alongside the desk. He said, "Russ, I need you to sit behind this desk for the next three weeks. Your first order of business is to find me a top-flight secretary, plus an outstanding first-level supervisor for yourself. We will then be a team of four—to pull off this major executive development session for President Easlick. The reason I want you to sit behind my desk is because I will be on vacation for the next three weeks studying for the Michigan State Bar Exam. I graduated from evening law school last month."

I said "I can do that." I had twenty-three years of diverse management experience in a variety of positions. I had taught the Dale Carnegie course for six years, and was currently teaching a business management course, evenings, for Wayne State University at the General Motors Technical Center in Warren, Michigan. Plus, this work is what I enjoyed doing the most.

Ken left on vacation. I lucked out, first finding Joanne Arsineau, a division-level secretary. She arrived. Executive Vice President, David Wenger, had sent Ken a note suggesting that he consider Carol Miller when he put together his conference staff. She wanted to return to Michigan Bell after staying home for twelve years to raise her daughter. Dave's take was that Carol had been an excellent Chief Operator whom he had known many moons ago. Dave was right. Carol came on board in a first-level supervisory position. We were off and running, although our leader was doing legal stuff for the next three weeks.

One step at a time. We decided on fourteen weekly sessions. Each week was to begin at 2:00 P.M. on Monday. This was to be a live-in conference. With the involvement of our conference bureau, we selected the Troy-Hilton Inn located directly across the I-75 expressway from the already-selected conference location at the newly completed Michigan State University Management Education Center.

This facility contained a fifty-seat (desk type) amphitheater, perfect for seeing and hearing. The voice assist speaker system was top-of-the-line.

The plan was to have the first of the fourteen week-long meetings begin the first Monday of October, 1977, with thirteen additional sessions in available weeks going forward. All conferences were to be completed at the end of the first week of February, 1978. This allowed for down-time for holidays and room for any other necessary adjustments. One cancellation was needed due to a snow storm. Thus the fourteenth session ended in mid-February.

Ken was reporting to Richard (Duke) Barron AVP. With Ken gone, Duke guided me in establishing the conference topics, along with recommendations for a proper presenter for each topic. When asked to participate they all said "maybe".

The "executive" group: District, Division, Assistant Vice President, Vice President, Executive Vice President, totaled about 500 men and women. Total company employees at that moment in time was 31,000. Total management employees 9,000. Weekly seminar attendees would be between forty and fifty in number. Each department was assigned a proportionate number of seats to fill each week. It was truly an interdepartmental conference, just as president Easlick had requested.

By the time our leader, Mr. McLarty, returned from vacation, we had moved well along the PERT chart. The conference site had been selected. Lunch and dinner menus had been arranged, as well as locations for both. Michigan Bell departmental speakers needed to be lined up for presentations each week for the fourteen weeks ahead. Several would need Ken's high-level arm twisting. He obtained commitments from each presenter. Hotel rooms were reserved, amenities ordered, hospitality suite was set up. The local tennis house agreed to special late evening reservations for court time.

The conference bureau, working with the printing department, was deep into preparing signage for a variety of needs, including large conferee name plates on slabs of Styrofoam for placement in front of each conferee's desk, so who was who could be read from the podium. The programs were designed, awaiting completion of the list of presenters. When requested, we assisted our in-house speakers with special effects, e.g. slides, videos, charts, graphs, and handouts. There were plenty of these. State of the art slide synthesizers were in use. Rear screen projection was universal. Both the photographic and art work was outstanding. We pushed for the list of presenters to be completed so the programs could be printed.

It took time and negotiations to line up speakers from the outside world. I remember some: Neal Shine (Executive Editor, *Detroit Free Press*), Doug Ross (Michigan Director of Commerce), Joseph Tushinsky (Consumer Advocate), Ralph Nichols (President, Dale Carnegie Associates—SE MI), the owner of a vineyard in western Michigan (friend of an MBT officer). Each speaker was asked to develop their talk on the theme of service to customers, no matter the industry. The length of talks was not stipulated. None lasted more than forty-five minutes. There were also several other presenters. Speakers spoke after lunch, which they ate seated next to Ken McLarty or me.

One of my tasks was to meet the president every Friday when he arrived just before lunch.

Each particular day's menu was always the same. This was OK, as the conferees were all new each week. That first Friday, I met Dave and filled him in on what was happening. I warned him that the entrée was Chicken Kiev, and to beware of the spurting butter. I had been warned by Chef Steve that one needed to be very careful cutting into the Kiev, as it would be loaded with hot butter. You guessed it. Dave cut into the chicken with gusto and a dime-sized spot of hot butter reached the center of his tie and spread quickly. He wiped it away, saying "you warned me." A hovering waitress handed him another dark green napkin. Michigan State colors for an "M" man. The butter spot did not go away. He later mentioned that event good naturedly from the podium.

Each of the fourteen conferences went well. Feedback from conferees was exemplary. The long hours of planning, rehearsals, adjusting, and being willing to make changes on the fly made for success. Behind the scenes there were a few glitches. We used numerous Kodak slide carousels. At night they were locked up in the projection room behind the big screen. However, somehow the carousel prepared for Public Relations AVP Don Gillard's presentation that first week was used by a group renting the facility for the evening. Michigan Bell had the entire venue rented by day. The slides had been removed from the carousel and piled in random order on the projection platform. In a panic we called the photographic department and explained. They rushed from Detroit to Troy, where the conference was located. They brought a large light board to fit all sixty slides, and used the original sequence list to put it all back together a few minutes before their boss, Mr. Gillard, was ready to begin clicking the slide projector. Had he found out that his staff had failed to number the slides, he would have not been pleased. Our lips were sealed.

Our staff was not perfect, either. That first Monday morning, as Carol Miller was unpacking the large name plates pasted on Styrofoam backings, she noticed a conferee's name was misspelled. It was AVP Paul Hines, spelled Paull with two "l's." She crushed the sign, tossed it in the trash and called the conference bureau for a quick print up and delivery of a "corrected" name card by 2:00 P.M. Carol will forever have to live with the fact that this was the way Mr. Hines spelled his given name—Paull. His proper name plate arrived in time, just like the slides had done. Paull never knew.

The conference ended each week on a high note. President Easlick, now always with a clean tie, spoke after lunch as the finale to a busy week.

His message summed up the conference around his stated objectives. He put all 31,000 employees into the mix. His final admonition to these high-level leaders was; *"The thrills in life come from when you help people, not from when you hurt them."*

Ken McLarty was for certain the conference director. He was at the podium directing traffic, introducing speakers, and summing up many times each week. I was at the back of the amphitheater, at the ready for whatever needed attention.

It was interesting to watch how conferees reacted to the variety of activities.

Two division managers had their in-baskets delivered every morning. Then, hiding behind their large name plates, they completed a review and gave the pack back to the courier. One division manager sat in the front row and trimmed his finger nails. The clicks could be heard, picked up on the very sensitive microphone. I never saw anyone sleeping or eating. Good groups—mostly.

Three times, Ken opted out of being in front of the group for the day. He took over rearguard duty, and sent me to the podium. That was fun.

These fourteen weekly sessions ended. Our team of four spent the next two weeks preparing the final report in miniscule detail, ending up with more than seventy pages. Dave Wenger delivered this document to his boss, the president. They were both delighted with the report and the positive feedback from their many subordinates. Our leader Ken McLarty gave us carbon copies of his notes to President Easlick regarding our performances over those past eight-and-a-half months. My very positive assessment of Carol Miller went along with his offerings.

It is amazing even now to remember that Division secretary Joanne Arsineau was thereafter promoted to a first-level supervisory position in Personnel, Carol Miller to a second-level position in Labor Relations, Ken McLarty to Assistant Vice President and soon transferred to AT&T in Chicago, and I to a full third-level district manager's position in Personnel. My title: District Manager Succession Planning.

The next year, President Easlick requested a second President's Conference. It was put together by AVP Earl Ross and Manager Julie

Height, plus two other staff members. I attended that conference as a conferee. It was very well done, and shorter by one day, as we had recommended. This new team had the advantage of having been attendees at that initial conference, plus they had our seventy pages of details to go by. They did not need to develop a PERT chart.

◊

DISTRICT MANAGER—SUCCESSION PLANNING: 1978

It took twenty-three years, seven months, and twenty-two days to reach my original goal of being a full third-level manager at the Michigan Bell Telephone Company. My district was a new one, small and a bit unusual. It was named "Succession Planning." The purpose was to gather corporate-wide personnel data, analyze these massive findings in a particular manner, draw conclusions, then prepare and deliver statistically supportable recommendations on having the right management replacement ready when needed. These were not my strengths or particular interests. However, I was fortunate to have a great staff with abilities to get things done and done well.

My entire staff was on loan: Dave Sweet, a manager from Business Offices (previously Commercial); Nancy Byrum, a manager from Operator Services (previously Traffic); Carol Dennard, a supervisor from Human resources (previously Personnel); Ardella King, a district secretary from operator services; and as it turned out, most importantly, Debbie (surname not remembered), a twenty-four-year-old recent University of Michigan graduate with a Master's Degree (MS) in statistics. Her energy was seemingly unlimited. In my view she was a mathematical genius.

Our first involvement was a trip to an AT&T-conducted training conference at a Company facility in Kansas City, Missouri. We all went. This was obviously an AT&T-directed project, "to insure, that into the future there would exist managers at every level, in every company, who have the knowledge, skill, and experience to successfully carry on the business." All of that seemed to fit that long-time Bell Telephone "promote from within" philosophy. We learned, we took copious notes, and we picked up all available handouts.

We returned to home base ready to do it. Dave and Nancy would report to me, as would secretary Ardella. Carol would report to Dave. They would be responsible for negotiating with all departments for personnel records to include all second-level and third-level management personnel, plus assembling the records for summarizing. Debbie would report to Nancy. They would be responsible for analyzing each management level by department, and assembling all existing skill banks, by gender, race, age, education, length of service. Then Debbie would statistically "age/season" the data to include projected retirements, mortality rates, promotions, and transfers within the Bell System, and other losses. The need to alter personnel systems going forward should then be obvious, we reasoned, initially and ongoing.

This was going to take some time to accomplish, test, and verify. It was decided to publish a one-page update bulletin for monthly distribution to second-level managers and above. This project was not seen as threatening, and it *was* non-threatening, but interesting, and important to all going forward. We had much classified information—e.g. which senior officers were not college graduates. We kept all information to ourselves.

The "Succession Planning Bulletin" was created. It gave facts, no opinions.

Nancy was the publisher. She said that meeting a monthly publication deadline was the pits. She did it, and did it well.

When I was transferred to this assignment, I reported to Tom Fezzey for a second time. From the beginning I had heard rumors that this assignment was to get me promoted, now or never. I was, after all, fifty years old. I had been passed over on more than one occasion when it appeared that I was the better prepared candidate. My performance (or non-performance) at management assessment, concluding that I lacked aggressiveness, had probably not been helpful to my cause. As it turned out, the rumor mill had my promotion finally arriving because my management training credentials were the best; plus, I could be counted as an example of non-age discrimination under the Equal Employment Opportunity Commission (EEOC) guidelines. I never thought I would fall under government guidelines. However, if true, I appreciate the help from Uncle Sam.

As it turned out I had been "parked" for eight months in the succession planning slot, awaiting an opening in the Management Training and Education District. Then along with a variety of other moves, I reached my dream job "district manager—Management Training and Education." The moves that got me there? Betty Jean Jefferies left the EEOC district responsible for handling claims of discrimination. She was replaced by my former boss in management training, Hoyce

Wrather. This opened up the management training job for me. Nice.

The succession planning group continued through completion of the project. Dave Sweet led it to conclusion. Ongoing maintenance of the data became part of the Human Resources department record-keeping. I was learning my new assignment and lost track of that great staff. Not certain how long Debbie and her MS degree stuck around the Phone Factory.

The management training district office had moved from the Bell Building to an office on Twelve-Mile Road and Pierce in Berkley, Michigan. Training was being delivered in two large conference rooms and four suites in the Troy Hilton in Troy, Michigan, Fifteen-Mile Road and Stephenson Highway. For the first time in my career I lived within one mile of my office and two miles from the training site. Over the next eight years in this position, the location would change from time to time. My high interest in this position never changed.

☙

DISTRICT MANAGER—
MANAGEMENT TRAINING: 1979

I had reached my goal. I was transferred from the Succession Planning district to my dream job: heading up the Management Training and Education district. Interestingly enough, the "Education" moniker had been tacked on at some point, even though nothing seemed to have changed with the curriculum or responsibilities.

During the next eight years I would report to nine different leaders. This fact brought some good news with it. I was empowered to make decisions involving management training design, development, delivery, and funding, because these many new bosses did not come fully equipped with the knowledge and skills to do so. I loved making these decisions. On average, I had a new boss every 10.6 months, during my long tenure as Director of Management Training. For whatever reason, the "Education" part got dropped and the "Director" piece added. Nice sound to that.

Here is the chronology of my leaders, as my work unfolded: reported to Jack Knaff, division manager; he retired. Reported to Tom Fezzey, division manager; he went off to the Cleveland Clinic for some heart repair. Reported to Richard (Duke) Barron, AVP; he went off to AT&T to prepare to become CEO of a new marketing (sales) group. Reported to Dave Wenger, VP & GM, until a new AVP could be arranged (circa two and a half months). It was quite an experience meeting with Dave in his office, with bone china tea cups for the coffee brought in by his secretary, along with tasty little biscuits. Reported to Martha Thornton, AVP. Reported to Jim Coates, division manager; he left quite unexpectedly and I never found out where he went. Reported to Jim Wilkes, AVP, who replaced Ms. Thornton; Jim went on special assignment. Reported to Dick Christie, AVP. And finally, I reported to Kathie Carrick, AVP. Through it all, the management training team continued to design, develop, and deliver what in my opinion was a group of quality courses to large numbers of first-level and second-level management employees representing every department. Plaudits regarding our courses kept coming. We humbly accepted all of them.

Also worthy of mention is that during the period just after the AT&T divesture was announced on January 1, 1984, my then leader was hell-bent on dissolving the management training district. This attempt was thwarted in two ways: we quickly began offering one-day and two-day seminars in problem-solving techniques, presentation skills, and other mini-courses. These offerings expanded our presence. Demand for seats in new course offerings burgeoned. And, even more important, leadership for all training, both technical, and management, was slowly but surely being considered for transfer to Ameritech headquarters at Hoffman Estates, Illinois, near Chicago. The Antitrust case against AT&T had resulted in divesture into seven regional companies, referred to as "Baby Bells." Ameritech was one of these babies, and Michigan Bell was part of that group of five companies.

Beginning in May 1984, district-level training managers from the five operating companies comprising Ameritech—Michigan, Illinois, Ohio, Wisconsin, and Indiana—met with Ameritech executives to plan the transfer of training responsibilities and budgets from the five operating companies to what was now being referred to as "Ameritech Corporate." Two mornings each month for almost two years, 1984 and 1985, Bill Davis, representing technical training at Michigan Bell, and I, representing management training, boarded an American Airlines early-bird flight to Chicago at 7:15 A.M. Gaining an hour, we were able to arrive on time at Ameritech's temporary headquarters in an office plaza on the outskirts of Chicago. A bit different: we were picked up at Midway airport by a young woman driving a dark green Jaguar with tan leather seating. She was a division secretary. She never failed to be there. Neither Bill nor I had ever ridden in a Jag. Hence as we were racing (and I mean racing) along the expressway, she said, "Oh my, I guess I am running out of gas." Thankfully she explained further; "I will have to switch to the other tank." She reached somewhere on or under the dash and flipped a switch. Bill and I breathed easier. Never too old to learn about modern-day foreign autos.

Success for district managers in all departments depended on the staff they were fortunate enough to inherit and subsequently develop and maintain. This is undoubtedly true in all organizations. The difference in the Management Training group was that instructors (second-level managers) were all transfers into the training organization on a two-year rotational basis. Managers were usually willing to transfer. Many sought the opportunity, as I had. They learned to teach several courses, help update and often design new course materials, plus teach numerous demanding sessions over that two-year assignment. They then returned to their departments, wiser and more ready, willing, and able to contribute their newly-honed leadership skills.

I remember the people who were in the training district during my eight-plus-year tenure fondly and I will appreciate them forever. Precisely what years each manager was there and some names are not recalled. The list below is meant to show the departmental diversity of the group. These different company backgrounds, in my opinion, gave the instruction added strength. In no particular order: Bob Herta, Treasury; Ruth Brown, Business Office; Julie Height, Business Office; Theresa Steiber, Comptroller; Judy Gant, Business Office; Al Orloff, Construction; Verne Jones, Plant; Al Chaddick, Plant; Mary VanDeventer, Personnel; Jerry DeVoogd, Marketing; Carolyn Field, Operator Services; Bill Baker, Personnel; Larry Altamaro, (uncertain); Paul Greening, Business Office; Nancy Gordon, Public Relations; Dave Stader, Comptroller. Two managers were "hires from the street" whom I do remember and will mention later. Only two registrars covered those eight years—Carol Schufeldt and Ken Grunow. Four district secretaries were employed during that same period—Chris Sineveck, Peggy Wagner, Marie (surname not recalled), and Mary (surname not recalled). Part of my not remembering is due to the fact that turnover in district secretaries was quite brisk. Peggy Wagner had the longest tenure as secretary with the training district.

During a long career in a company that you respect and enjoy being a part of, you get to know many of your peers and bosses. Relationships and events surrounding them create many memorable moments. One never-to-be-forgotten event was with Dan Grady. During most of my time in the management training organization, Dan was Vice President of Personnel. He was there when the name of his department was changed to "Human Resources."

I had first met Dan and his wife Margaret socially. They were friends of Bud and Rita Smith. Bud was Chief of Photography for General Motors Corp. My wife Ginny and I knew them from PTA activities in Royal Oak. Bud and Rita gave parties galore. We were invited, along with the Gradys. As Dan's career sped along, he was forever bugging me for lagging behind. He knew me well enough to know that my goals were different than his. Dan had been a "four-star" student in the University of Detroit business school. He knew I was an MBA evening division graduate from that institution. We were both friends and admirers of Father Farrell, the long-tenured dean of the Business College.

Fast forward to Dan's Michigan Bell Vice Presidency and my district level position in management training. Dan loved numbers. Remember, he was three levels above my pay grade. However, on several occasions he had his secretary set up an appointment with my secretary for him to visit our training site at the Northfield Hilton, Fifteen-Mile Road and Stephenson Highway, in Troy. He would arrive from his home in Grosse Pointe, Michigan at 7:00 A.M. sharp. We would have a light breakfast in the hotel dining room.

I would be ready with the numbers I knew he was interested in reviewing—the full list of courses currently being offered, additions and deletions from the previous year, the number of conferees in first-level and second-level management courses year to date, the number of women and minorities completing each course. Plus, details on any new offerings under development. He usually had suggestions, and sometimes questions he wanted me to explore and answer for him. All my bosses were OK with Dan's visits. They knew him well.

During one early morning meeting, Dan and I were talking while standing looking out the plate glass windows at the rear of the second-floor classroom. Having finished breakfast, we had gone to the classroom. Dan was always interested in conversing with students once they were assembled for the class. Dan Grady had a high-end sense of humor, and an engaging chuckle to go with it. As we stood conversing, looking out the window, a Lincoln Town Car pulled into a spot facing the building. Instructor Ruth Brown alighted. Dan recognized her. Soon a Mercedes pulled in next to Ruth's auto. Instructor Judy Gant alighted. Dan did not know her. A few minutes later a Corvette arrived. Instructor Julie Height struggled out of that low-slung vehicle. Dan knew her. Smiling, Dan opined "maybe we are paying our managers too much money." Then came his one-of-a-kind chuckle. He did not stay at the window long enough to see instructor Al Orloff, whom he also would have known, park his ten-year old Pontiac in the second row next to instructor Bob Herta's vintage (I think) Ford

Fairlane. He knew Bob well. Seeing them would have been reason enough to laugh even harder. Dan was then introduced to the assembled class of students, all of whom were managers. He enjoyed a lengthy question and answer session with these conferees.

My promotion, in March 1978, had made me the 329th district manager in the Michigan Bell Telephone Company. Thus, all district managers were part of the top 428 management employees. With all employees totaling circa 31,000, this meant we district managers were in the top 1.4% of the work force. District managers seemed to be more connected to each other than other levels in the organization. Many of my peers believed this was true because we were a definable entity. Second-level managers were too large a group, and division and above managers were too small a group for either to be fraternal. District managers readily exchanged information to help each other succeed. The majority of us were already where we wanted to be, so backbiting was not in vogue. Of course, some wanted to move further up the line, no problem with that, and those who didn't were usually willing to help those who did. We all had several good district level friends to palaver with on a variety of business issues, and beyond.

I had a few special buddies; Maury Brackenbury, Bill Rice, Ginny Merritt, Fred Gaulsetti, Doris Gabrys, John Hill, Don Burwell, Pete Grylls, George Fezzey, Mac McVicar, Bill Davis, Chuck Woodhead, Tom Warth, Ed Mabin, Tom Fezzey, Bob McQuiggin, Dave Beamer, Howard Zuidema, Len Bender, Len Weil. This group included several who went out of our ways to arrange a one-on-one lunch at least twice each year, usually at the same eatery. Examples: Maury Brackenbury, at Stouffer's on Washington Boulevard, in the Men's Grill located at the rear of the restaurant, with the red leather booths. We usually got there just after 11:30 A.M. and had to endure watching the manager inspect every waitress. First their hair; then fingernails; and finally, the bow on their aprons. When they left for their posts, the most attractive ones remained behind in the Men's Grill. I usually had the same luncheon selection: minced tongue sandwich with dill pickle and iced tea—"lots of ice." Cannot remember Maury's selections. This "men only" culinary venue was later opened up to women.

I met Bill Rice quite often in the back room at Nemo's Café across from the Detroit Tigers' Ball Park, at Trumbull and Michigan Avenue. Deluxe Burger, thick slab of onion (when no afternoon meeting was scheduled). Often joined there by George Fezzey, and occasionally by his brother Tom, who was a division manager. We often played pool on the coin-operated table in that back room. Don Burwell was a forever faithful lunch partner in April and September. He would call to set up a date. He always insisted that he buy at his "club," the Engineering Society of Detroit in the Rackham building. Great food and ambience. I accepted. However, with Don and some others I would also take them to "my" club, a luncheon-only operation at the top of the Buhl building in downtown Detroit. The "Savoyard Club" was named for the river that runs under Detroit skyscrapers. This eatery had been operating for many moons. The hostess, Polly, had been working there for fifty years. The food was marvelous. I paid the $20.00 monthly dues out of my own pocket. I did have one Christmas celebration breakfast there for the training district staff.

Don Burwell and I had some things in common. We both moonlighted, although I did not do so after I became a district manager. Don taught English at the University of Windsor. He pastored a storefront Christian Church in Highland Park, Michigan, my hometown. Plus, he was pursuing a Ph.D. at my alma mater Michigan State University. I think his advanced degree was to be in business management.

Ed Mabin and I met for dinner only twice, both times in his hometown of Kalamazoo, where his office was located. Both times I was there on a training mission for the Operator Services district. Ed was a member of the "Beacon Club" near or at the airport. Having dinner there was for members and their guests only. Very nice accommodations, at what I would call a high-end restaurant. I never did get him up to Club Savoyard. Ed also moonlighted, but not for money. He was deeply involved with his alma mater, the University of Michigan, in assisting the Registrar's office in recruiting and retaining minority students for the University. The last time I saw Ed was at a departmental meeting at the Amway hotel in Grand Rapids. This was a Business Office's departmental planning meeting. Dick Holtcamp was the department head, along with his division managers, Evon Murphy and Joe Valicevic. This was a serious work meeting, planning for the next year. Participants received a very nice ballpoint pen printed with "Joe and Evon." There was only one major entertainment, a high-end professional magician, name well known then, now forgotten. Those were the glory days at Michigan Bell. The magician's fee was $35,000.00. Lee Stevens, conference bureau supervisor, let that contract and had the paid invoice in her center desk drawer.

Chuck Woodhead and I lunched and exchanged information often, usually at Nau's Snow-White restaurant on Grand River between Six-Mile and Seven-Mile Roads, probably in Farmington. I had reported to Chuck briefly when I was a college trainee in the Webster/Kenwood district. He was an interesting study in management style, very deliberate, and in my opinion, very effective.

Chuck believed strongly in the motto *"supervising and managing is teaching."*

He loved to tell the tales of his two encounters with the Equal Employment Opportunity Commission, I think both times with a Judge Green and his staff (Same last name as the Federal Consent Decree judge later on). Chuck was the district manager in Webster/Kenwood at the time. The EEOC inspectors scheduled visits to Michigan Bell offices to ensure adherence to the letter and spirit of Equal Opportunity laws. These inspections included recruiting records, training records, promotions, plus demotion and dismissal records. The final inspection activity was an interview with the district manager. Chuck was asked how many minority employees he had working in the district. Chuck answered truthfully, "I do not know." The two days of inspections ended. When the written report wended its way back to his division manager, it contained a critical paragraph regarding Chuck's lack of knowledge as to the number of minority employees in his group. It ended with a question; "How can Michigan Bell expect to improve the Corporation's minority profile if managers do not know how many minority employees are on the payroll?" Chuck was asked by his division manager, Bob Harrington, to correct this deficiency going forward. He agreed to do so.

Fast forward three years. Chuck Woodhead had been transferred to the Ann Arbor district. Judge Green and his EEOC team are now inspecting suburban and outstate offices. The same routine as in the Detroit office three years earlier. The final interview with the district manager (Chuck) included a question phrased a bit differently than before; "How many minorities are on your payroll?" Chuck was ready with specific details, including Asians and even one Pacific Islander, the husband of a University of

Michigan graduate student. The final report eventually arrived at Fort division headquarters. Chuck was taken to task again. This time, the report ended with the question "How can Michigan Bell expect to treat all employees equally if leaders are counting the numbers of those in each race?" His division manager had not changed; it was still Bob Harrington. So, in Chuck's words, "he had his day in the tank again." This time, however, he received just a smile, a handshake, and a "hang in there" from his boss. Then they went to Snow-White's for lunch.

It came to pass, over time, that four of my colleagues disappeared, three without saying goodbye. The exception was Ed Mabin. He left suddenly when we all were at that departmental meeting in Grand Rapids. However, he called me a week later to say goodbye. He was applying for a job with a firm named Jacobson's, I think in Lansing. Bob McQuiggin just plain disappeared, as did Mike Jordan, although Mike and I later ran into each other in a Publix supermarket in St. Augustine, Florida, and found out we were in the same gated community on the ocean. He owned and lived there all year round in a condo. We had a three-month lease. We played duplicate bridge with a large group, occasionally at the same table.

I didn't ask, and he did not tell me why he left MBT before retirement time. We had been cohorts since we had taken IBMC together at the Fort Shelby hotel thirty-three years earlier. We had originally met because we were both friends of Murray Merrill.

Don Burwell and I had had lunch at the Engineering Society of Detroit in December, not sure of the year, and then he was gone. District managers were a close group, but on occasion we were also closed-mouthed. Understandable—I guess.

During my eight-year tenure as Director of Management Training and Education, I had two opportunities to make presentations on the eighteenth floor of the Bell Headquarters building, where the vice presidents and the president worked. The first opportunity came in 1979. We were in the process of updating the second-level manager Advanced Management Skills course. Departmental training coordinators wanted to learn more about the new course components. The meeting was to be held in the "Round Room."

When AT&T elected David K. Easlick president of the Michigan Bell Telephone Company, one of the first things he did was to arrange for a new executive conference room to be built just outside the senior officer's quarters on the eighteenth floor of the Bell headquarters building. The conference room was unique in that it was round. It contained a massive round table with sixteen comfortable chairs. Dave's idea was that when discussions were held and decisions were being made, it would help the process if every participant was on equal footing, with no one at "the head of the table."

So, there I was at that round table. My presentation was planned for ten minutes, with five minutes for questions. Personnel vice president E. Daniel Grady had arranged the meeting with several department heads. I was just wrapping up the presentation, preparing for questions, when the double doors opened and President Easlick came in and sat down. I found out later that he was looking for Dan Grady. I said, "Welcome, David. We are just wrapping up a review of revised instructional objectives for the second-level manager's course." He responded, saying, "is that like the consultants we hire, when they tell us, at the end of their intervention, what will have happened or will happen in the future?" I said, "a perfect description of an instructional objective. Thank you for that. Any questions?" There were none. Dave signaled to Dan. They left.

As the group broke up, I talked to several of the departmental personnel managers. There were questions after all. They concluded that "when the president sits down at the round table, it automatically becomes oblong, and he is then seated at the head." That was my only official visit to the round room.

My other official visit to the eighteenth floor was for a presentation to a Board of Directors meeting in the Board Room. The year was 1980. The antitrust division of the federal government was heating up rhetoric regarding a so-called AT&T monopoly. The AT&T legal department, along with their corporate training organization, had developed a one-half day course to be presented to all management employees in the Bell System. The purpose was to explain what behaviors needed to be avoided so as not to give the appearance of monopolistic practices. This was the course that Jack Schuler, chief counsel for Michigan Bell, had contacted me to ask the Management Training group to plan, organize and deliver, along with an attorney from his staff. The course had a ten-minute video that was very well done. It supported the training guide. In all, it was very teachable material. Don Brown was the lead attorney for this project. He co-trained most of these sessions with one of our staff members, often Al Orloff. I did one session in the Flint district, testing the material in real time.

The plan was for me to have a ten-minute slot on the Board's always-packed agenda. I would not use the video, but rather three slides. The boardroom was outfitted with a rear-screen projector and a new wireless clicker. There would be one handout, a duplicate of the slides' talking points. Howard Zuidema was the corporate Secretary (a fourth-level position). He had been mentoring Board of Director meetings since long-ago when then-president Bill Day had promoted him to that post. He made all arrangements for my visit. He would set up the slides, as the new rear screen feature was tricky. He would also introduce me. He did, with more plaudits than I deserved. But why not? Howard and his wife Adeline were part of the sixteen-member potluck group that we had belonged to for many years. Another Bell management employee held forth in that same social group as well: Len Bender of the Comptroller's Department, and his wife, Paulette.

My charge was to review with board members the contents of the course which was intended to alert management personnel to the many dangers of appearing to be a monopoly. I remember only one item: *Never discuss a piece of telephone equipment or service which was "in the pipeline" but not yet available to customers.* This was because a customer might delay their purchase of said item from one of our competitors, and be willing to wait for the same-or-more-advanced item from AT&T, Western Electric, or one of the Bell operating companies. The point was that the equipment or service might never materialize, but the competitor's sale would have been squelched.

My ten minutes of fame ended. There were a few questions, mostly legal questions, thankfully directed to chief counsel Jack Schuler, who was at the other end of the table. Mr. Zuidema had counted out the proper number of handouts for each side of the long table. He started them along both sides. The board member nearest to me shook hands and said "very interesting." I said "thank you." That was my first and last time in the Boardroom.

Three managers from our management training group were assigned to deliver this one-half day course, along with two attorneys. They travelled the state in tandem to assembled districts from all departments. Conference room arrangements, including video availability plus class member lists, were prepared by our registrar, Carol Schufeldt. Travel and lodging accommodations were put together by Lee Stevens from the Conference Bureau. The plan was to minimize travel and lodging expenses. It was decided that the upper peninsula personnel would travel to Saginaw for the training. They were used to that. These training sessions were rated by conferees as "very interesting."

Two years later the Bell System was torn asunder when AT&T CEO Charlie Brown signed Judge Harold Greene's consent decree. Our major training effort regarding antitrust considerations had not stopped the inevitable. However, the management trainers had enjoyed the experience of delivering the course, especially co-training with an attorney. They had together delivered forty-six sessions statewide.

Beginning in the spring of 1984, it became impossible to make a deal with any department in the company to release a manager for a two-year assignment with our Management Training organization. Not knowing what divesture would bring regarding personnel availability, all departments were sitting tight. Michigan Bell continued to promote from within, and almost never "went to the street" to fill management vacancies. Our management training district had been in the throes of being eliminated, as mentioned above. However, we were granted permission to hire two managers from outside, to train to become instructors. General personal district manager John Conway vetted applicants. It was my responsibility to make the final selection to hire. My first selection was a young woman with solid business experience; a five-year graduate of Central Michigan University. She accepted the position conditionally; if her application to the Peace Corps was "validated" within two weeks, she would be going to Costa Rica, not joining Michigan Bell. It was. She went. Back to Mr. Conway asking for more candidates.

Before any more interviews were scheduled, I received a call at home from VP Dan Grady. It was Wednesday evening, June 4, 1984. He asked me if I would be willing to take the next day off. I figured something was up. It was. He was committed to deliver a Class Day address at Harper Woods North High School on Friday evening, June 6; he had been called to a command performance meeting at AT&T, 195 Broadway, New York, N.Y. Impressive. The meeting was regarding the recently enacted divesture. Would I deliver the talk? I said yes. He said, "I knew you would. A courier is on the way to your home with the script and all necessary instructions. Take Ginny with you. Take tomorrow to prepare. Your boss has already agreed. Knock 'em dead, babe." I did it. The school board president presented me with a brass letter opener engraved: R.S. Vahlbusch, Harper Woods N. HS., 6-6-84.

All great fun for me, and Ginny too. Dan was appreciative.

I wish I had known better than to even consider going to the street for second-level management instructors. I should have just increased everyone's teaching load and gone back into the classroom myself. Telephone people were a special breed, and the inbreeding kept us strong and focused. Plus, I should have realized that successfully interviewing and selecting prospective hires requires special expertise. I for certain did not have that necessary knowledge, or the interviewing skills. Nevertheless, I selected and hired two instructors. They were the two biggest mistakes of my long career. One was totally inept in front of the group, though did possess minor course design skills. One was acceptable as an instructor, although had way too much hubris (vitamin "I") to be at all effective with experienced Bell management employees. I recommended dismissal of the "totally inept" employee. I had assembled ample documentation for this action (half a credenza full). However, my leader at the time had some personal performance issues and was not willing to take on any more controversy. What happened to my two "errors in judgment" is unknown to me. I suppose, one way or another, they both got melted into the Bell System.

It was the spring of 1987. I was fifty-nine years old. My time was up as Director of Management Training. It had been a great run. Eight glorious years leading a fine staff of instructors, course developers, registrars, and secretaries. I was to be transferred back to my home department, Commercial, by then renamed "Business Offices."

Lee Wallace was appointed director of management training. She had been promoted twice since she was one of my supervisors in the Mechanization Methods group, in Dave Beamer's district back in 1969. At some point Lee had begun working in Paull Hines' organization. I am not certain about the department. I also lost track of how Ameritech finally decided to manage technical and management training in the new company. The plan Bill Davis and I had helped develop during those early morning sojourns to Chicago was to transfer the director of management training from Indiana Bell to an Ameritech office in-or-near Chicago, thus eliminating four district-level management-training directors. I never found out if that plan was implemented.

My personal plan was to work until age sixty-two. My new assignment would be a great opportunity to go out quietly in just under three years. It worked out to be just under two.

☙

DISTRICT MANAGER—S.R. TRAINING—TELEPHONE SALES: 1987

My new leader was division manager Evon Murphy, rumored to be incredibly well organized, and oh! 'twas true. She led the Residence organization reporting to AVP Dick Holtcamp. Division Manager Joe Valicevic led the Business organization, also reporting to Dick. My responsibilities included continued development, plus ongoing management, of the centralized training unit that provided initial training (IT) to newly-hired Service Representatives. Classes were being conducted for both Order and Billing SRs from the three metropolitan Detroit divisions: Fort, Gratiot, and Woodward. In addition, I was to manage a recently formed Telephone Sales Group located in Port Huron, Michigan. Continuation training (CT) was still the responsibility of each individual district.

This all looked interesting, especially because of the great peer group which was Ms. Murphy's team: Fred Gaulsetti, Bill Rice, Ginny Merritt,

Doris Gabrys, Ed Mabin, John Hill, and Russ Vahlbusch, all experienced district managers, with a wide variety of responsibilities. Monthly division meetings were a delight to attend. Plus, the catered buffet lunch of soup, salad, and make-your-own sandwiches was an added attraction. We continued the meeting during lunch.

SR training had forever been delivered in every district, by supervisors often rated as very good at that job. When SR force turnover was high, there was often a need for two training supervisors per district. This usually meant one to train billing SRs, and one for Order SRs. Each class consisted of two newly hired employees.

Thus, with a total of six districts in these three divisions, there could be up to twelve supervisors providing training at one time. However, this seldom occurred. Usually there was down time. Then these imbedded training supervisors acted as relief supervisors within the district organization. This was thought not to be an efficient use of supervisory and training dollars. Under the centralized plan, training would be conducted in just three locations utilizing six supervisors in full-time training positions. Thus, there had been a force reduction of circa four instructors. I can remember only one of those instructors, Jane Hoker, from the Townsend business office.

I visited each training classroom three times. The first time, I welcomed the newcomers and told the company story that I had heard from my first district mentor, Earl Morrow, thirty-three years earlier. It was the concept of the three-legged stool, as practiced by Michigan Bell (AT&T as well). *Treat every "leg" — Customer–Employee–Shareholder — with care and respect. Favoring one group over the other unbalances the entire organization.*

New employees usually agreed, and said so.

The second visit was two weeks into the training cycle (three weeks of training for Billing SRs, and four weeks of training for Order SRs). On those occasions, I presented my own homegrown explanation of why standards were high regarding the accuracy and completeness of information being given to customers via the Bell telephone. It went like this: in school, if we were 75% correct on tests, quizzes, and answers to classroom questions, we would receive a passing grade, probably a "C." In the world of business, if we were incorrect or incomplete 25% of the time, we would not stay in business very long.

The difference was that in school we did not have handbooks with all the answers at our disposal, nor would the teacher answer any question we had while we were taking tests or quizzes. In Michigan Bell business offices, we have a well-designed, up-to-date handbook for reference, plus a supervisor (teacher) nearby to answer any question we might not have been able to find in the handbook. Just do not guess. With these two resources always available, expectations for accuracy and completeness should rise to a level between 99.5% and 100%. It always took a bit of discussion on each point, but in the end at least tacit acceptance was reached with these young women. In those days, no men occupied those positions. Obviously, the purpose of this description was to sell the use of reference materials and the supervisor's expertise, thus giving Michigan Bell Telephone customers the most accurate and complete service possible. That was the goal.

The third and final visit I made was to hear and discuss the SR trainees' responses to the quiz they had taken a day or two earlier. In an effort to make centralized SR training the best it could be, I had devised fifty-question true-or-false quizzes for both Order and Billing classes. Questions were based on errors and irregularities catalogued by the corporate observing staff during the previous three months. All discrepancies had been recorded on a Form forever called an SO-5. What those letters and digits stood for I don't remember.

I was allowed to review the SO-5 forms from the six Detroit districts. I wrote fifty questions for Order SRs and fifty for Billing SRs. Basing these questions on actual failed customer contacts seemed like a good way to connect new SRs with the real world. Any lack of understanding in these areas would allow re-training to occur before these new hires began taking live customer calls.

Analyzing several hundred SO-5 documents took a morning at the headquarters building in downtown Detroit. Then out for lunch at Stouffer's on Washington Boulevard. I went with a friend, Bill Rice. My usual lunch partner at Stouffer's, Maury Brackenbury, had retired. The "Men's Grill" sign was gone. We still headed to the back room where it used to be. The red leather booths were still there, now all occupied by women. No men in sight. We settled in and ordered. The minced tongue sandwich was still on the menu. A waitress I remembered from the old days took our order. I asked how the changeover from the "men-only" past was going. She responded by saying, "It's OK. The ladies are nice, but the tips are a great deal smaller." That's progress.

SR trainees responded positively to this testing. They got to correct their own test. The training supervisor then reviewed each question. Thus, if the student had missed a question, they were immediately aware of it. Misses per test averaged four (8%). Training supervisors were pleased with the opportunity to review and correct without causing students to feel that they were being put on the spot. Usually the students readily admitted their misunderstandings. My final visit also included discussing their upcoming challenges in the real world of work. Handshakes all around. Centralized SR training was working. There were a few glitches centered mostly on the fact that more than one-half of the trainees would be working in offices other than where they had been trained and done some live work, out in the main office. For the most part practices and procedures were the same, office to office. However, each office, over time, had developed a few local "ways of doing things." Those were ironed out rapidly and the "centralized" SR training system was moved along.

The other portion of my new district was a group of sales personnel located on the second floor of the accounting building at 112 Grand River, Port Huron, Michigan. This team was supervised by a young woman whose name I have forgotten (maybe Jean). I am sorry about that. She was very good at her job. She lived fifty-five miles away from Port Huron. She was always on time, and frequently worked beyond quitting time. The team had three separate work activities. The first was that a few Bell Telephone advertised products and services contained a telephone number ending up in the automatic call distributor, a machine, in this office. In some respects, the distributor may have been a forerunner to a "robocaller." Calls arrived and were distributed to an available representative, who was trained to discuss, sell, and place an order for the product or service.

These same team members also made a small number of unsolicited calls to residential customers to sell certain services and equipment. At the time, this was a test to see what could be done in the area of direct telephone selling into the future. The last topic for this group to handle was the final elimination of four-party-line telephone service statewide. All eight-party-line service had been eliminated, but there were still a few pockets of four-party service around rural Michigan. These customers had been notified by mail that a call was coming to change their service. The goal was to sell one-party service. It was not easy to convince customers to go from four to one. Most settled for two-party service, even with some solid sales effort.

I visited the Port Huron facility twice each month. Everything ran smoothly.

The supervisor should have been a second-level manager, but efforts to make that happen went nowhere. We did put together a performance package for her which gained her a hefty bonus for the year. I don't remember the amount.

It was now October 1988. At my Stouffer's luncheon with Bill Rice, we had discussed retiring. We both were approaching thirty-five years of continuous Bell Telephone service. I knew Bill was on a special assignment. He was located on the mezzanine surrounding the main lobby of the Bell Headquarters building. He had a staff of one—Joanne Arsineau, who had been promoted to a first-level supervisor's position in the Human Resources department after the President's Conference circa ten years earlier.

When I tried to shake Bill down at lunch as to what he was doing, he was mum. However, as we parted he said; "don't go off half-cocked, and retire, for a while at least."

Bill's admonition turned out to be good advice. I knew him well enough to know that he would never divulge a corporate secret; but in his parting shot there had been a warning. On November 1, 1988, the hint turned into reality. The Management Force Adjustment Program (MFAP) was announced. An unknown number of management employees received offers under this plan. The purpose for downsizing the management force most assuredly had many facets. Ameritech had been formed as a leaner organization. The number of districts was being diminished. Getting rid of a management force at the top of the pay scale was good business. If one did not accept the offer to retire, they would face the future not knowing where they might be assigned. Plus, it was hinted that if a position was not found, you "might" be retired without any "extra help." The extra help offer was this: one year's base salary (opportunity to spread it over two years for an obvious tax advantage), plus full medical coverage for you and your family until age sixty-five. Then at age sixty-five, a company-paid-for medi-gap policy until death. In Evon Murphy's division there were five takers, beginning with Evon herself. In alphabetical surname order, the four district managers were Doris Gabrys, Fred Gaulzetti, Virginia Merritt, and Russ Vahlbusch. There were twenty-nine other management employees who accepted the company buyout at the end of the year 1988.

Before you signed the papers and walked them up the stairs out of the high-domed lobby in the Bell Building at 444 Michigan Avenue, Detroit, Michigan, to the mezzanine where Bill Rice and Joanne Arsineau were waiting to process them, there was yet another very important decision to be made. This was the first year that you could choose a "lump sum" instead of a pension (annuity). The rub was that the amount of the "lump" depended on the current interest rate. The higher the interest, the lower the lump. Interest at that time was, I think 8.0%. This meant that the lump sum would be comparatively small.

One year later the interest rate had dropped. The summing up was much larger.

I had taken the "for-as-long-as-I-live monthly pension check" (with a 10% penalty to give wife Ginny one-half of my pension under the "joint and survivorship" provision). At the time of this decision, the Harris Bank in Chicago was handling AT&T pensions, at least for the Mid-West. The total AT&T pension escrow fund at that time was 4.2 billion dollars. I reasoned that pension payments were quite secure into the future. Interestingly enough, because I have been retired for so long (thirty years), if I live one more year, my pension income over thirty-two years in retirement will have surpassed my income from my more than thirty-four working years at MBT. Amazing.

It was a long walk up those stairs carrying retirement papers. I would be retiring thirty-four years, five months, and 24 days after I had waited for Earl Morrow in his Webster district office to begin my career at the "Phone Factory" or with "Ma Bell" or whatever other, affectionate moniker we might lay on our longtime employer. We were all scheduled to leave on December 30, 1988. In the event there were any slipups, a day of grace was built in to make corrections. The way accounting was set up, all MFAP retirees needed to be gone before January 1, 1989. Thus, our salaries and benefits would not need to be logged into the new year's budget. Payouts could all be billed to 1988. Our group of five made it off the payroll on time.

There was one last optional offer with the MFAP retirement package. That was an opportunity to receive six months of assistance from an outplacement organization named Jannotta Bray & Associates.

This relatively new service had sprung up as major organizations, e.g. AT&T, Stroh's Brewery, General Motors, and many others began downsizing management and occasionally non-management employees. The service was to help voluntary retirees, forced retirees, or dismissed employees to reenter the job market.

☙

CONSULTANT—JANNOTTA BRAY & ASSOCIATES: 1989—1996

There was a time when wife Ginny and I had daydreamed of living in a small college town with ivy-covered red brick halls, and red maple trees lining the sidewalks as students returned from summer break. I would be teaching at the college or university. That did not happen. However, when I retired at the end of 1988 nearing the age of 61, I had hoped to be an adjunct instructor at a nearby institution of higher learning.

Teaching at Lawrence Technological University in Southfield, Michigan seemed like a good idea. Originally located in my hometown of Highland Park, Michigan, the university's name had been changed from Lawrence Institute of Technology (LIT) to Lawrence Technological University (LTU). I selected this venue because I had gone to high school with the then-president Richard Marburger, Ph.D. (physics). He and I had worked together on many of our high school class reunions, his class 1946 and mine 1945.

In addition, I had support from Robert Harrington, whom I had known and done work for in the Fort division office at Michigan Bell. He was a retired MBT Assistant Vice President, now working at LTU as chief fund raiser for the Foundation. In addition, working for Bob was a former Michigan Bell district manager, now retired, M.J. Morrell. I applied for an adjunct teaching position in the College of Business.

However, even with all that firepower in back of me, I did not become an adjunct instructor at the university. This was because I wanted to teach fall term, and summer school, if needed. The Dean of the College of Business wanted me for both fall and winter terms—and I did not want to teach in the winter. We parted friends, and Ginny and I went to Florida for the next nine winters. It made sense for him not to have to hire two people to fill one slot, although I was disappointed.

So, when that plan ended, I decided to take advantage of that part of the Michigan Bell MFAP offer regarding outplacement services from Jannotta Bray & Associates. I signed up for the four-day training session, scheduled for the third week of February, 1989. I completed the course. At the end, as is usually the case, a form was circulated asking for an evaluation of the course, both the materials and the instructors. As I had understood it, by the end of the four days we would have a viable resume, the draft of a cover letter to send with the resume, plus a generic draft of a job solicitation letter. We would also have learned the boiler-plate stuff, like networking and how to respond convincingly to questions during interviews. In my opinion we had not reached these objectives.

I did not fill out the evaluation sheet, but rather took it home and thought about it for a while. Then I sat down at a typewriter (did not have a computer in those days), and prepared a comprehensive answer to those evaluation questions. At the bottom of the form it said; "Signature not required." I signed.

My evaluation was very negative, although not quite scathing. I rated the instruction as barely satisfactory. However, I conceded that, with the existing course design and training materials, maybe no one could have delivered a satisfactory course. I made a few suggestions, and mailed the form to the Michigan president of Jannotta Bray—Ms. Joan Hanpeter. She had kicked off the training session I had attended. I then began to reshape my resume and associated letters to begin my job search in earnest. I still wanted to work.

Two weeks into preparing for my new job search regimen, I contacted my old boss, Nancy Hernandez, at Wayne State University. There were no openings. However, the next day I received a call from Jannotta Bray of Michigan. The president's secretary asked if I would be available to meet with her boss Ms. Joan Hanpeter someday during the upcoming week. Yes. A date, day, and time was set. I went.

Joan Hanpeter was a very gracious person. She definitely had her hand on the pulse of the outplacement market. She was interested in knowing more about my tenure with the Michigan Bell management training group, plus my work with Dale Carnegie and Associates and Wayne State. Interestingly enough, at the end of our interview, Joan offered me a full time position as an outplacement consultant. I tactfully declined, explaining that I was looking to be a part-timer, so I could go to Florida during the winter for the next few years. I explained how the Lawrence Tech situation had gone down in flames. I then bravely made her a counter-offer.

I would teach the four-day outplacement seminar. However, before I did that, I would do a complete rewrite of the course. When done, I would ask her to get the entire staff together for a day to go over my offering, line by line, to make needed additions, changes, and deletions, so that the finished product would include everyone's input, including hers. The goal was to be the best we could be. She agreed that we would do this.

We did it and more. The group billed $1 million the next year. Each member of the team received a brass pencil holder engraved "Thanks a Million." Joan's offer had been $300.00 per day, to move up to $400.00 per day after six months. That was fine with me. I knew that I would enjoy the work at any price.

I worked on the training upgrade at home, only going into the office to drop off and pick up typing from the typing pool folks. The total project, including multiple testing of each segment, took six months. My daily fee increased to the agreed amount. I began to teach groups of outplaced employees from a variety of mostly large corporations. I had already conducted instructor training sessions for everyone on our team of five instructors. I also travelled to other Michigan cities where corporations were downsizing (sometimes they preferred to use the term "right-sizing"). Usually this was the first time in their long-storied histories they had used an outplacement strategy. This was really fun for me and wife Ginny, as Jannotta Bray paid for spouses to travel with employees who were working away from home base. We even had two different assignments with companies in her hometown of Battle Creek.

Our team dealt only with outplaced employees in the annual salary range off $50,000.00 to $125.000.00. Other teams at Jannotta Bray handled lower and higher salary levels. We met our instructional objectives. At the end of the four days, every conferee had a viable resume plus draft letters of transmission, appreciation, and exploration. Each conferee had participated in a one-on-one realistic mock interview, and had dealt with the nine most-often-asked questions by Human Resources job interviewers. All aspects of the job search were covered in miniscule detail. Great emphasis on the why and how was placed on contacts and networking. Each conferee had also participated in a videotaped mock interview. During the video playback, the interviewee was able do his or her own critique, with guidance from the instructor if needed.

I continued working with Jannotta Bray for seven years. I had taken Social Security at age sixty-two, so I could only earn $7,800.00 dollars per year before those earnings would decrease my

Social Security payout. I stayed at or below that earnings figure on principle, not wanting to pay the penalty for exceeding the earnings ceiling. Wife Ginny and I went to Florida each year as planned. Thus, I was able to continue doing a bit of teaching, which I enjoyed. And I made a few bucks, first as an independent contractor, and then as a Jannotta Bray employee. The corporation changed to that format for some unknown reason.

In the spring of 1996 Jannotta Bray became "Right & Associates." They were bought out by this much larger organization. The use of part-time instructors was about to come to a halt. Not to worry. Ginny and I were moving forty-three miles east of Royal Oak to a retirement community in New Baltimore, Michigan. Timing is everything. I decided to really retire. The thought of an eighty-six-mile round trip to work was much too daunting for this sixty-eight year old. I had been working for sixty-three years. What a grand run it had been.

ՁՅ

AFTERWORD

This has been a sampling
of tales that could be told.
Many will forever remain untold.
The work had made possible
a lifetime filled with play
and good works.

Perhaps there will be a sequel—

"Playing My Way Through Life."

The Author
Chippewa Falls, Wisconsin
April 2, 2020

☙

ACKNOWLEDGEMENTS

This book was written because our two sons, Eric Stearns Vahlbusch, Attorney at Law, and Dean Jefford Bristol Vahlbusch, Ph.D., were interested in knowing about my time in the United States Army, especially Korea.

After a couple of attempts to get that project underway, I decided that the work I had done leading up to being drafted, the work I did in the Service, and the work I did afterward—mostly with the Michigan Bell Telephone Company—constituted a good way to frame the military portion of my working life. Hence *Working My Way through Life* was conceived.

Initial and subsequent edits were accomplished by boutique publisher Mary Catharine Nelson, of "Ideas into Books," Kingston Springs, TN. The final edit was by son Jeff.

Wife Virginia Luan Vahlbusch (née Bristol) listened as I read every chapter of my rough drafts to her. She pointed out duplications and, whenever I failed to explain where I was at each moment in time, geographically, she was the first to spot it. Even more importantly, every time I threatened to quit writing, it was Ginny who would not hear of it. She got me back to working the keys on my laptop.

Together everyone helped make me a published author again at age 92, circa ten years after I published my first book: *Don't Give Up Give Back—Remembering Pat Heenan.*

Russ Vahlbusch
Chippewa Falls, Wisconsin
April 2, 2020